P

GERALD VIZENOR

MANIFEST MANNERS

Narratives on Postindian Survivance

UNIVERSITY OF NEBRASKA PRESS
LINCOLN AND LONDON

⊚

First Bison Books printing: 1999

Library of Congress Cataloging-in-Publication Data
Vizenor, Gerald Robert, 1934–
Manifest manners: narratives on postindian survivance / Gerald
Vizenor.
p. cm.

ISBN 13: 978-0-8032-9621-3

1. Indians of North America—Social conditions.   2. Indians of North
America—Public opinion.   3. Public opinion—United States.
4. Indians of North America—Ethnic identity.   5. Indians in literature—History and criticism.   6. American literature—Indian
authors—History and criticism.
I. Title.
E98.S67V58   1999
970.004′97—dc21
99-38527   CIP

The order, the strength, the economic power are there. The heart trembles in front of so much admirable inhumanity.

ALBERT CAMUS, American Journal

To dissimulate is to feign not to have what one has. To simulate is to feign to have what one hasn't. One implies a presence, the other an absence.

JEAN BAUDRILLARD, Simulations

The signifier of the racial discourse has no referent in the material world. It arises within whiteness as an attempt to sustain wholly artificial limitations, thus it gestures vaguely toward the real world without ever touching upon it, though the material effects of its manipulation are undeniable.

ALDON LYNN NIELSEN, Reading Race

The four races of humanity. Mix red, yellow, white and black together and you get brown, the color of the fifth race. This is a natural ordering of things. It therefore seems natural to me to work with all races, each with its own special meaning, identity and message.

RUSSELL MEANS, Mother Jones

Writing is not destined to leave traces, but to erase, by traces, all traces, to disappear in the fragmentary space of writing, more definitively than one disappears in the tomb, or again, to destroy, to destroy invisibly, without the uproar of destruction.

MAURICE BLANCHOT, The Step Not Beyond

Preface

Gerald Vizenor

Native American Indians are the originary storiers of this continent, and their stories of creation, sense of imagic presence, visionary memories, and tricky survivance are the eternal traces of native modernity.

The first two names convey the historical creases of cultures, continents, and nations; the third name, *indian*, misgiven here in italics, insinuates the obvious simulation and ruse of colonial dominance. Manifestly, the *indian* is an occidental misnomer, an overseas enactment that has no referent to real native cultures or communities.

Manifest manners are the course of dominance, the racialist notions and misnomers sustained in archives and lexicons as "authentic" representations of *indian* cultures. Manifest manners court the destinies of monotheism, cultural determinism, objectivism, and the structural conceits of savagism and civilization.

Survivance is an active sense of presence, the continuance of native stories, not a mere reaction, or a survivable name. Native survivance stories are renunciations of dominance, tragedy, and victimry. Survivance means the right of succession or reversion of an estate, and in that sense, the estate of native survivancy.

The simulation of the *indian* is the absence of real natives—the contrivance of the other in the course of dominance. Truly, natives are the storiers of an imagic presence, and *indians* are the actual absence—the simulations of the tragic primitive.

The postindian, an urgent new word in this book, absolves by irony the nominal simulations of the *indian*, waives centuries of translation and dominance, and resumes the ontic significance of native modernity. Postindians are the *new* storiers of conversions and survivance; the tricky observance of native stories in the associated context of postmodernity. The *indian* is a primitive simulation; postindian narratives observe natives, the chance of totemic associations, conversions, and reversions of tribal cultures, as postmodern survivance and vivancy. Native stories are cues of modernity. "Cultural changes, such as the one that gave birth to the modern age, have a definitive and irreversible impact that transforms the very essence of reality," wrote Louis Dupré in *Passage to Modernity*. "Not merely our thinking about the real changes: reality itself changes as we think about it differently. History carries an ontic significance that excludes any reversal of the present."

Dupré explained that a "nominalist theology" and an archaic, creative humanism are the "borderstones" of modernity. The divine was separated from nature in the late fourteenth century, and at the same time, the stories of creation changed. Cultural meaning was converted by this "removal of transcendence." So, instead of "being an integral part of the cosmos, the person became its source of meaning." Reality was separated into two spheres, the human mind, as the source of meaning, and nature. This, he pointed out, "marks a new epoch of being."

Disquieted thinkers, however, and "entire schools of thought critical of the modern fragmentation have attempted to reverse the effects by returning to premodern premises." Natives, then, were the curious, colonial prey of this pastorly return to the cruces of premodernism: missionaries translated native stories as moralistic themes of primitive transcendence, and much later, the federal government established boarding schools in the nineteenth century to remove the "primitive" by teaching the new realities of market economies, wage labor, property, and provident modernity.

The Renaissance was a humanistic revival of art, literature, commerce, individualism, and privacy. Natives, too, praised the presence of distinctive identities in sacred names, nicknames, and stories. Meditation and vivacious memories created virtual, totemic associations that were incomparable; no two visionary names could ever be the same, a source of inimitable *individual* identities. Stories were never the same either; oral stories arose as imagic memories, not as the mere recitation of liturgy.

"Modernity is an *event* that transformed the relation between the cosmos, its transcendent source, and its human interpreter," argued Dupré. "Some traditional societies feeling threatened by modernity have attempted to defend themselves against it by often violent reversals to the past. Such rearguard actions are not likely to prevail. Science and technology have become inevitable and practically indispensable for survival."

Jean Jacques Rousseau issued the romantic simulation of the "noble savage," the bright, untutored men of nature, to counter the onerous corruption of society. François-René de Chateaubriand likewise construed a "primitive liberty" in the romantic solitude of the savage and nature.

Postindians and natives come together in the stories of human motion, the ontic significance of cultural conversions, presence, and modernity. Natives are the storiers of *actual* motion and, at the same time, the *visionaries* of transmotion, the motion of creation, imagic memories, and totemic associations; ontic, or real existence, and a phenomenal existence of the senses. Decidedly, the stories of human motion and the virtual conversions of animals and humans are native modernity.

Natives have always been on the move, by chance, necessity, barter, reciprocal sustenance, and by trade over extensive routes; the actual motion is a natural right, and the tribal stories of transmotion are a continuous sense of visionary sovereignty.

Many natives were the past masters of trickster stories and, in that aesthetic sense, always prepared to outwit missionaries, social scientists, and manifest manners; trickster stories tease creation, nature, conversions, simulations, and sacred ceremonies. Trickster stories are suspensive, the natural reach of reason and survivance; the traces of stories, in this sense, are cultural conversions and native modernity.

Native stories are an imagic presence, the actual tease of human contingencies, but *indians* are immovable simulations, the tragic archives of dominance and victimry. Manifest manners favor the simulations of the *indian* traditionalist, an ironic primitive with no cultural antecedence. Postindians absolve the simulations with stories of cultural conversions and native modernity. *Manifest Manners: Postindian Warriors of Survivance* was first published five years ago. The subtitle has been changed in this edition to *Narratives on Postindian Survivance*, a consideration of the historical strategies and theoretical style of my essays. The first paperbound edition pictured on the cover an artistic representation of Russell Means, a reproduction of a silk screen portrait by Andy Warhol. This new edition includes an introduction, and the original cover art, "Wild West Show," is by David Bradley.

Karl Kroeber reviewed *Manifest Manners* for *Common Knowledge*. "Seeking to recover 'the genius of natural reason, the ironies of tribal imagination, and the shimmer of survivance stories' from the surveillance of the social-science mentality, Vizenor affirms the comic delight in chance and coincidence manifest in oral cultures. Proving himself our subtlest analyst of 'postindian' conditions, Vizenor skewers 'kitschymen' and wannabees who profit from pandering to the thieves of tribal realities by manufacturing commercialized concoctions of tricksterism, as fraudulent as the authenticities of docudrama."

A. Robert Lee pointed out in his critical essay, "The Only Good Indian is a Postindian? Controversialist Vizenor and *Manifest Manners*," that "Vizenor's insistence on taking over, or rather taking back, the English (the American?) language which *ab initio* has pre-empted Indianness, and whether in spoken or written script. 'We must represent our own pronoun poses in autobiographies,' Vizenor argues, and be about the 'imagining of ourselves.' This, thereby, will be to counter the English language's dispossession and appropriation starting, he implies, with the very word 'Indian.' The span, again, can or rather should, be as various as need be, running from oral-aural invention to script, from music and the visual arts to dance, from high seriousness to humor, from a voicing of the Natives in the city as much as on the reservation. In this Vizenor joins James Baldwin, writing in

1964, in his call for the operative language to be 'made my own,' to 'bear the burden of my experience.'"

Tom Lynch reviewed *Manifest Manners* for the *San Francisco Chronicle.* Gerald Vizenor "exhibits his imaginative literary and cultural criticism and refuses to conform to the limits of the essay genre. In some cases the essays may be better thought of as critical poems, engulfing the reader in a swirl of images and linguistic play." Lynch pointed out that the language of postmodern exposition may "convey a sense of elitism at odds with the egalitarian and human concepts" that underlie the theories.

The concept of manifest manners first came to mind about thirty years ago. I was then director of a federal desegregation program at the Park Rapids High School in northern Minnesota. The strategic point was to reduce the high dropout rate among native students who were bused to the consolidated school from the nearby White Earth Reservation. I conducted regular training sessions for teachers, bus drivers, and others, in an effort to change the conditions that caused so many bright native students to leave school before graduation. Most of the native students had earned high grades in reservation schools and had scored above average on national standardized tests.

The Park Rapids High School teachers were wise, dedicated, generous, and sensitive to native students; nonetheless, they expressed some of the most obvious racial notions. For instance, many teachers, who endorsed the idea of "cultural deprivation," thought that natives were not as capable of abstract reasoning as other students. I named their "educated" views, manifest manners.

Native educators likewise contributed to manifest manners, and did so with a curious crease of authenticity. I had invited an outstanding native educator to meet with the reservation students; she told them that *indians* "do not touch each other." That notice, naturally, prompted a humorous response, but the students truly wanted to know what *indians* she was talking about. She had written as much about cultural values in her dissertation, and at many education conferences, advanced the idea that *indians* were not touchers. Many teachers *embraced* the "no touch" notion to answer an apparent *indian* reticence in public school, and the rest is manifest manners.

The teachers might have learned more from the journals of Meriwether Lewis and William Clark than from the "no touch" native educator with a doctorate. Lewis was eager to meet natives, and, when he first contacted the Shoshone, reported that the native men "advanced and embraced me very affectionately in their way which is by puting their left arm over you[r] wright sholder clasping your back, while they apply their left cheek to yours and frequently vociforate the word *âh-hi-e, âh-hi-e* that is, I am much pleased, I am much rejoiced. bothe parties now advanced and we wer all carresed and besmeared with their grease and paint till I was heartily tired of the national hug." The selection is from *The Journals of Lewis and Clark*, edited by Bernard DeVoto, based on the *Original Journals of the Lewis and Clark Expedition*, edited by Reuben Gold Thwaites.

Lewis and Clark were unexpectedly threatened by the *absence* not the actual presence of natives on their expedition. Lewis noted that "we begin to feel considerable anxiety with rispect to the snake Indians. if we do not find them or some other nation who have horses I fear the successfull issue of our voyage will be very doubtfull or at all events much more difficult in it's accomplishment." Some two week later he wrote in his journal, "I was overjoyed at the sight of this stranger and had no doubts of obtaining a friendly introduction to his nation provided I could get near enough to him to convince him of our being whitemen." Lewis and Clark are honored in this book.

Luther Standing Bear, three generations later, boarded a train for an expedition in another dimension and direction; he was born to be a warrior and became one of the first native students to attend the federal school at Carlisle, Pennsylvania. He graduated, taught school on the reservation, toured with Buffalo Bill's Wild West show in Europe, and wrote several books. "I always wanted to please my father," he wrote in *My People the Sioux*. "All his instructions to me had been along this line: 'Son, be brave and get killed.' This expression had been moulded into my brain to such an extent that I knew nothing else." He noted that his father "made a mistake. He should have told me, upon leaving home, to go and learn all I could of the white man's ways, and be like them." Luther, a name selected at random at the federal school, had "come away from home with the intention of never returning alive unless he had done something brave."

Standing Bear was a postindian warrior who had encountered the enemies of native cultures with wit and courage, countered the manifest manners and conceit of dominance, and created his own stories of survivance. He is honored in this book.

The superintendent of the Wahpeton Indian School in North Dakota, a federal boarding school, encouraged a few of his best students to dance in dyed chicken feathers to the music of the Lord's Prayer. I was a journalist at the time, and the superintendent, a retired military officer, was eager to show me how much the school supported *indian* traditions. He summoned a lonesome native child to dance for me in the gymnasium. I was shamed by the spectacle, but decided not to undermine the dance. The simulations, chicken feathers, and *indian* traditions were manifest manners.

Marge Anderson, the honored chief executive of the Mille Lacs Band of Ojibwe Indians in Minnesota, observed in the *American Indian Report* that Ojibwe, or *anishinaabe*, "tradition speaks of peace among the four colors—red, white, yellow and black— which represents the four races on earth. Sadly, some people in this world don't show respect for all races, and they hurt others through their lack of understanding."

Sadly, the notion of four racial colors perpetuates a crude separation of humans and cultures rather than begetting a sense of peace. Marge Anderson, a generous native leader, surely never intended to advertise racialist theories. The notion of four colors as a native tradition insinuates polygenesis, or the partite creation of humans, and a return to premodernism.

William Warren, the *anishinaabe* historian, observed more than a century ago that some native creation stories were told as a dubious courtesy to missionaries. "These tales, though made up for the occasion by the Indian sages, are taken by his white hearers as their *bona fide* belief, and, as such, many have been made public, and accepted by the civilized world," he wrote in *History of the Ojibway Nation*. The Great Spirit, in one of these stories, created three races: white, black, and the red race. To the first he gave a book, denoting wisdom; to the second a hoe, denoting servitude and labor; to the third, or red race, he gave the bow and arrow, denoting the hunter state." These tricky creation stories were translated and treasured by some missionaries at the time. "We have every reason to believe that America has not been peopled from one nation or tribe of the human family, for there are differences amongst its inhabitants and contrarieties as marked and fully developed as are to be found between European and Asiatic nations—wide differences in language, beliefs, and customs." Warren teases native creation stories and sustains a literary modernity.

Carolus Linnaeus, the eighteenth-century naturalist, devised a binomial nomenclature for plants and animals, and he also classified humans into "five natural categories." Four of the racial divisions were "geographically based," wrote Barbara Katz Rothman in *Genetic Maps and Human Imaginations*. Linnaeus observed these characteristics: *Homo sapiens Americanus*, red, harsh face, wide nostrils, scanty beard, obstinate, free, and ruled by custom; *Homo sapiens Asiaticus*, yellow, melancholy, greedy, haughty, severe, and ruled by opinion; *Homo sapiens Afer*, black, lazy, flat nose, silky skin, and ruled by caprice; *Homo sapiens Europaeus*, white, serious, strong, with blond hair, blue eyes, active, very smart, inventive, and ruled by laws; and *Homo sapiens Monstrosus*, those curious and strange humans.

Linnaeus represented three "natural categories" of the modern human species with racial detractions, ruled by custom, opinion, and caprice; those ruled by laws, the sapiens white, he vested with care and fair countenance. The last category was monstrous.

The United States Immigration and Naturalization Service, provides five similar categories to determine the "race" of applicants for citizenship: American Indian or Alaskan Native, Asian or Pacific Island, Black, White, and Unknown.

Race is a simulation, and the "science" of race is political not biological; human differences are genetic, but the notions of four races are dubious traditions and faux science.

"We are not separate species," observed Rothman. "Race was a liquid concept," but the once common metaphor of *blood*, as thicker than water, blue, red, hot, or cold, has lost significance. "No longer visible, no longer divisible, race has moved inward

from body to blood to genes; from solid to liquid to a new crys-
tallization," she argued. "Blood no longer tells. Race is now a
code to read; the science of race is the science of decoding."

Russell Means, the brave dancer, radical spiritualist, errant
reservation politician, presidential candidate, postindian movie
actor, and cruces of *indian* simulations, has his own notions of
race, reason, and culture. "Humans are able to survive only
through the exercise of rationality since they lack the abilities of
other creatures to gain food through the use of fang and claw,"
he pointed out in his autobiography, *Where White Men Fear to
Tread.* "But rationality is a curse since it can cause humans to
forget the natural order of things in ways other creatures do not.
A wolf never forgets his or her place in the natural order. American Indians can. Europeans almost always do."

Means argued that he does not care about skin color, and, at
the same time, notes that white is a race and "one of the sacred
colors of the Lakota people—red, yellow, white and black. The
four directions. The four seasons," and the "four races of humanity." He described the brew of four colors as a fifth race.
"Mix red, yellow, white and black together and you get brown,
the color of the fifth race. This is a natural ordering of things."

Means, who has been named in many criminal warrants in
state, federal, and reservation courts, recently faced what must
be considered a postindian session of the Navajo Supreme Court
held at the Harvard University Law School. The *New York Times*
reported that the court convened "to hear an assault case against"
Means. "He is accused of beating his father-in-law in 1997 in
Arizona's Navajo Nation, but, as an Oglala Sioux, he asserts he
cannot be prosecuted by another tribe." Means had asked the
same court to review a paternity and custody case, about ten
years earlier, and consider a preliminary injunction of the Oglala
Sioux Court. He favored the jurisdiction of other native courts
at the time. "In the United States," he pointed out in *Where White
Men Fear to Tread,* "courts of similar jurisdiction operate on a
principle called comity. That means courts of one state recognize the jurisdiction and validity of others. Indian courts on different reservations are bound likewise."

"Ishi Obscura," my essay on the simulations of that native

man who never revealed his sacred name, concludes with mention of his death and apparent cremation on March 25, 1916. Recently, an investigation revealed that Ishi's brain had been excised for "scientific examination" during an autopsy at the University of California, San Francisco. Orin Starn, an anthropologist at Duke University, and research historian Nancy Rockafellar, confirmed that Alfred Kroeber had given the "preserved brain" to Ales Hrdlička, a physical anthropologist at the Smithsonian Institution.

The University of California, San Francisco, reported in an electronic daily that the autopsy was "standard procedure" at the time, but not the excision of his brain. "Until Rockafellar and Starn completed the investigation, it remained unclear whether the brain had been stored elsewhere or cremated with the rest of Ishi's remains. The cremated remains currently rest in an urn" at Mount Olivet Cemetery in Colma, California.

The *San Francisco Chronicle* reported that "Rockafellar was disturbed by the discovery. She said that what happened to Ishi was 'a morality tale' for scientists and physicians." The Yahi people were exterminated in the late nineteenth century by savage miners and bounty hunters. Ishi was one of the last voices of a distinctive culture of native sovereignty.

Robert Fri, director of the National Museum of History at the Smithsonian Institution, writes in the *San Francisco Chronicle* that "Ishi's brain will be returned to his closest living relatives, the Yana people of the Redding Rancheria and Pit River Tribe. The Yana will then determine how to proceed with a proper burial." Fri points out that the "Smithsonian has followed both the letter and the spirit of the National Museum of the American Indian Act of 1989. This law, together with the Native American Graves Protection and Repatriation Act of 1990, reflects the moral principle that American Indians and Native Alaskans have a right to determine the destiny of their ancestral remains, sacred objects, funerary offerings and cultural patrimonial objects conserved in museums throughout the United States." Ishi was not his sacred name, but the return of his stolen brain and his imagic presence in our memories are measures of a native survivance.

Luther Standing Bear was on a train with other natives bound for the federal school at Carlisle, Pennsylvania. The train stopped in Sioux City. The "white people were yelling at us and making a great noise," he wrote in *My People the Sioux*. They "started to throw money at us. We little fellows began to gather up the money, but the larger boys told us not to take it, but to throw it back at them. They told us if we took the money the white people would put our names in a big book."

The "white people" are throwing even more money at natives today, several billion dollars a year, but the natives are at casinos, not at train stations. There are more than a hundred native casinos on reservations in the country. The Indian Gaming Regulatory Act recognizes an "exclusive right to regulate gaming" if the activity is not prohibited by federal or state laws.

My essay, "Casino Coups," argues that native governments must invest some of their casino riches to create embassies in various parts of the world, a strategic postindian presence, and then to negotiate the liberation of stateless families. For instance, the liberation and relocation of Kurdish, Tibetan, Haitian, and other families to reservation communities, would clearly sustain the moral visions and traditions of native cultures. Such diplomatic activities would be a wise, humane measure of native sovereignty.

Five years later, since the first edition of this book, there are no native embassies in other nations; not yet, but recently the Saginaw Chippewa Tribe of Mount Pleasant in central Michigan purchased a mansion on Embassy Row in Washington. The Newhouse News Service reported that the new "Saginaw Chippewa Government House is an elegant three-story building surrounded by power and influence," and located near the Vatican Consulate, the embassies of Norway, Finland, and Belgium. The money for the "purchase and renovations came from the tribe's profitable Soaring Eagle Casino and Resort in Mount Pleasant." Natives may throw some of their casino money back to elected and administrative officials over lavish postindian "dinner parties on Embassy Row."

Contents

POSTINDIAN WARRIORS

P resident Thomas Jefferson envisioned a water course to the western coast of the nation a decade before he proposed the expedition that would become the most notable literature of tribal survivance.

Meriwether Lewis and William Clark were instructed that the objective of their mission was to explore the land west of the Missouri River that "may offer the most direct & practicable water communication across this continent, for the purposes of commerce."

Lewis and Clark reported in their journal that they wanted to be *seen* by tribal people on their expedition. They were diplomatic at a distance, to be sure, and they were certain that their mission would have been threatened not by the presence of the other, but by the absence of the tribes.

Luther Standing Bear, three generations later, was on an expedition in another direction and dimension; he was one of the first tribal students to graduate from an eastern government school. He was curious and courageous in the presence of the other, and he was threatened by the absence of reverence, honor, and natural reason.

Standing Bear, Lewis, Clark, and others, created the simulations that would honor their survivance in literature. Simulations have never been uncommon in literature, as the simulations of the other are instances of the absence of the real, but these expeditions in at least two dimensions were more than the mere simulations of savagism and civilization.

The Lewis and Clark expedition was one of the first transcontinental encounters with diverse tribal cultures; the encounters were inevitable in the new nation, but the successive encroachments on the natural presence of the tribes were vicious and barbarous. The cruelties of national and colonial authorities were widespread; the grievous outcome of avarice, perverse determinism, and the destinies that would become manifest manners in the literature of dominance.

Lewis wrote in his journal on 18 July 1805, "as we were anxious now to meet with the Sosonees or snake Indians as soon as possible in order to obtain information relative to the geography to the country. . . ." Four days later he wrote that Sacajawea, the "Indian woman recognizes the country and assures us that this is the river on which her relations live, and that the three forks are at no great distance."

Lewis wrote on 27 July 1805, "we begin to feel considerable anxiety with rispect to the Snake Indians. if we do not find them or some other nation who have horses I fear the successfull issue of our voyage will be very doubtfull or at all events much more difficult in it's accomplishment."

Then, about two weeks later, he wrote, "I was overjoyed at the sight of this stranger and had no doubts of obtaining a friendly introduction to his nation provided I could get near enough to him to convince him of our being whitemen." The selections are from *The Journals of Lewis and Clark*, edited by Bernard DeVoto.

"Indeed, the greatest danger the Indians could pose for Lewis and Clark arose from their absence rather than their presence," wrote Larzer Ziff in *Writing in the New Nation*. "What was later to be a cliché in Western adventure fiction, the white man's seeing Indians and taking care to remain unseen by them, was reversed as they strained to see the Indians who they knew were seeing them in order to enter into dealings with them."

Lieutenant William Reynolds, in contrast to the earlier expedition of Lewis and Clark, remained *unseen* on the deck of the *Flying Fish*, a schooner in the first discovery expedition of the United States Navy. "We never saw any one for weeks, save a few Indians now and then who brought us Salmon and Deer and who were welcome enough, but as to Society, after a hard day's labour, we might as well have been in the great desert. We did long with all our hearts to see the face of some *human* creature," he wrote to his sister on 7 November 1841, after a survey of the Columbia River.

"Once in a great while we *did* manage to run up to Astoria and have a chat with the folks there, and sometimes we saw the young wives of the missionaries, pretty, rosy cheeked women, the very sight of whom gave us the heart ache. I am disgusted with all naked Indians and primitive people whatever, and shall be too happy . . . when I can associate again with the more intelligent and attractive portion of the human family, who carry ideas in their heads, wear clothes on their bodies and are fair to look upon." His aversion to the tribes would represent the racialism of the nation; in turn, that aversion to the presence of the tribes would become the cause of manifest manners and the literature of dominance.

Lewis and Clark traversed the same river thirty-six years earlier and were content to be *seen* by the tribes. Clark wrote in his journal on 24 October 1805 that the "nativs of ths village re[ce]ived me verry kindly, one of whome envited me into his house, which I found to be large and comodious, and the first wooden houses in which Indians have lived Since we left those in the vicinity of the Illinois. . . . Peter Crusat played on the *violin* and the men danced which delighted the nativs, who Shew every civility towards us. we Smoked with those people untill late at night, when every one retired to rest."

Standing Bear seemed to envision the onset of the postindian warriors of simulations; that sensation of a new tribal presence in the very ruins of the representations of invented Indians. "I always wanted to please my father in every way possible," wrote Standing Bear in *My People the Sioux*. "All his instructions to me had been along this line: 'Son, be brave and get killed.' This expression had been moulded into my brain to such an extent that I knew nothing else.

"My father had made a mistake. He should have told me, upon leaving home, to go and learn all I could of the white man's ways, and be like them." Luther had "come away from home with the intention of never returning alive unless he had done something brave.

"Now, after having had my hair cut, a new thought came into my head. I felt that I was no more Indian, but would be an imitation of a white man. And we are still imitations of white men, and the white men are imitations of the Americans."

Standing Bear was in the first class to attend the federal school at Carlisle, Pennsylvania. Later, he taught school on the reservation, witnessed the horror of the massacre at Wounded Knee, and toured with Buffalo Bill's Wild West show in Europe. This postindian warrior was active in tribal rights movements, an actor in several motion pictures, and he wrote several books about his experiences.

The postindian warriors encounter their enemies with the same courage in literature as their ancestors once evinced on horses, and they create their stories with a new sense of survivance. The warriors bear the simulations of their time and counter the manifest manners of domination.

Manifest Destiny would cause the death of millions of tribal people from massacres, diseases, and the loneliness of reservations. Entire cultures have been terminated in the course of nationalism. These histories are now the simulations of dominance, and the causes of the conditions that have become manifest manners in literature. The postindian simulations are the core of survivance, the new stories of tribal courage. The simulations of manifest manners are the continuance of the surveillance and domination of the tribes in literature. Simulations are the absence of the tribal real; the postindian conversions are in the new stories of survivance over dominance. The natural reason of the tribes anteceded by thousands of generations the invention of the Indian. The postindian ousts the inventions with humor, new stories, and the simulations of survivance.

Standing Bear, for instance, had graduated from the government school and he was working at John Wanamaker's department store in Philadelphia when he read in the newspaper that Sitting Bull, the Lakota healer, was scheduled to lecture in the city. "The paper stated that he was the Indian who killed General Custer! The chief and his people had been held prisoners of war, and now here they were to appear" in a theater. "On the stage sat four Indian men, one of whom was Sitting Bull. There were two women and two children with them. A white man came on the stage and introduced Sitting Bull as the man who had killed General Custer," which was not true.

Sitting Bull "addressed the audience in the Sioux tongue" and then the white man, the interpreter, misconstrued his speech in translation. "My friends, white people, we Indians are on our way to Washington to see the Grandfather, or President of the United States," and more was translated as the story of the massacre of General Custer at the Little Big Horn. "He told so many lies I had to smile."

Standing Bear visited Sitting Bull at the hotel. "He wanted his children educated in the white man's way, because there was nothing left for the Indian." The interpreter was in the room, so "I did not get a chance to tell Sitting Bull how the white man had lied about him on the stage. And that was the last time I ever saw Sitting Bull alive."

The postindian warriors hover at last over the ruins of tribal representations and surmount the scriptures of manifest manners with new stories; these warriors counter the surveillance and literature of dominance with their own simulations of survivance. The postindian arises from the earlier inventions of the tribes only to contravene the absence of the real with theatrical performances; the theater of tribal consciousness is the recreation of the real, not the absence of the real in the simulations of dominance.

Manifest manners are the simulations of dominance; the notions and misnomers that are read as the authentic and sustained as representations of Native American Indians. The postindian warriors are new indications of a narrative recreation, the simulations that overcome the manifest manners of dominance.

The once bankable simulations of the savage as an impediment to developmental civilization, the simulations that audiences would consume in Western literature and motion pictures, protracted the extermination of tribal cultures.

Michael Blake must have been cued to continue the simulations in his novel, *Dances with Wolves*. "There were Pawnee, the most terrible of all the tribes," he wrote. "They saw with unsophisticated but ruthlessly efficient eyes. . . . And if it was determined that the object should cease to live, the Pawnee saw to its death with psychotic precision."

The motion picture with the same name counts on the bankable manifest manners of the audience to associate with the adventures and discoveries of an errant cavalry officer who counters the simulations of savagism in *his* stories. The tiresome tantivy of tried and true horses with no shadows, and the Western tune of manifest manners, is the most serious deliverance of civilization ever concocted in the movies or literature. The Civil War has become one of those simulations in movies that abates the loathsome memories of more recent wars, and hastens the disabused heroes to discover their honorable pluck with native warriors. *Dances with Wolves*, for instance, must have been inspired by the men who heard the cicerones of *Broken Arrow* and *Little Big Man*. Manifestly, movies have never been the representations of tribal cultures; at best, movies are the deliverance of an unsure civilization.

Simulations are the absence of the tribes; that absence was wiser in the scenes of silence, richer in costumes, and more courageous on a ride beside simulated animals. Western movies are the muse of simulations, and the absence of humor and real tribal cultures.

"The absence of Indians in Western movies, by which I mean the lack of their serious presence as individuals, is so shocking once you realize it that, even for someone acquainted with outrage, it's hard to admit," wrote Jane Tompkins in *West of Everything*. "My unbelief at the travesty of native peoples that Western films afford kept me from scrutinizing what was there. I didn't want to see. I stubbornly expected the genre to be better than it was, and when it wasn't, I dropped the subject. . . . I never cried at anything I saw in a Western, but I cried when I realized this: that after the Indians had been decimated by disease, removal, and conquest, and after they had been caricatured and degraded in Western movies, I had ignored them too."

The Western movies, of course, are not cultural visions, but the vicious encounters with the antiselves of civilization, the invented savage. Since the national encounters over the war in Vietnam, however, the Indian is a new contrivance and encounter of the antiselves in postwestern movies. The new scenes of postwestern simulations are the melancholy antiselves in the ruins of representation; the tribal others are now embraced, a romance with silence and visions. The tragic wisdom that was once denied is now a new invention in such postwestern movies as *Dances with Wolves*.

The postindian is the new simulation in the postwestern salvation of the antiselves in the movies; the landscape, overrun to be sure, has turned even richer in postwestern movies with the rescue of natural reason and romance over the ministrations of antitribal mercantilism.

Wallace Stegner has ushered the postwestern landscape into a new theater of literary salvation and dominance; alas, he has no obvious need to be *seen* with the tribal others as survivance. "Being a Westerner is not simple," he wrote in his recent collections of essays, *Where the Bluebird Sings to the Lemonade Springs*. He observes that "ethnic and cultural confusion exists not only in Los Angeles but in varying proportions in every western city and many towns. Much of the adaptation that is going on is adaptation to an uncertain reality or to a reality whose past and present do not match. The western culture and western character with which it is easiest to identify exist largely in the West of make-believe, where they can be kept simple."

Thomas Jefferson, James Fenimore Cooper, Francis Parkman, George Bancroft, and other masters of manifest manners in the nineteenth century, and earlier, represented tribal cultures as the other; to them "language did the capturing, binding Indian society to a future of certain extinction," wrote Larzer Ziff in *Writing in the New Nation.* "Treating living Indians as sources for a literary construction of a vanished way of life rather than as members of a vital continuing culture, such writers used words to replace rather than to represent Indian reality."

The simulations of manifest manners are treacherous and elusive in histories; how ironic that the most secure simulations are unreal sensations, and become the real without a referent to an actual tribal remembrance. Tribal realities are superseded by simulations of the unreal, and tribal wisdom is weakened by those imitations, however sincere. The pleasures of silence, natural reason, the rights of consciousness, transformations of the marvelous, and the pleasure of trickster stories are misconstrued in the simulations of dominance; manifest manners are the absence of the real in the ruins of tribal representations.

Those who "memorialized rather than perpetuated" a tribal presence and wrote "Indian history as obituary" were unconsciously collaborating "with those bent on physical extermination," argued Ziff. "The process of literary annihilation would be checked only when Indian writers began representing their own culture."

Andrew McLaughlin and Claude Van Tyne, authors of a high school history textbook published by Appleton and Company a generation after the Wounded Knee Massacre, resisted the inclusion of more than about half a page on Indians. Manifest manners and the simulations of dominance are the annihilation, not the survivance of tribal stories.

"Simulation is no longer that of a territory, a referential being or a substance," wrote Jean Baudrillard in *Simulacra and Simulations.* "It is the generation by models of a real without origin or reality: a hyperreal. The territory no longer precedes the map, nor survives it." Americans, moreover, pursue a "more to come" consumer simulation, wrote Umberto Eco in *Travels in Hyperreality.* "This is the reason for this journey into hyperreality, in search of instances where the American imagination demands the real thing and, to attain it, must fabricate the absolute fake." Indians, in this sense, must be the simulations of the "absolute fakes" in the ruins of representation, or the victims in literary annihilation.

Wallace Stegner situates the western landscape in the literature of dominance. The land and new nation were discovered with nouns and deverbatives, consumed with transitive actions, and embraced with a causal sensation of manifest manners. The land was unnamed and became a place with names "worn smooth with use," he wrote in an essay. "No place is a place until things that have happened in it are remembered in history, ballads, yarns, legends, or monuments."

Stegner would never contribute to the annihilation of tribal cultures, but his concern over names pronounces that the land was untouched and unnamed in tribal stories. His pronominal discoveries of the land are the absence of tribal remembrance. He concedes to manifest manners in the cause of literature. "Plunging into the future through a landscape that had no history, we did both the country and ourselves some harm along with some good." Natural scenes with "no histories" are the absence of natural reason in the literature of discoveries. Tribal names and stories are real histories, not discoveries.

"We have made a tradition out of mourning the passing of things we never had time really to know, just as we have made a culture out of the open road, out of the movement without place," wrote Stegner. "No place, not even a wild place, is a place until it has had that human attention that in its highest reach we call poetry." His reluctance to honor tribal stories in the blood, land, and oral literature, the names and stories of remembrance, is the course of manifest manners; the christened names of discoveries and dominance.

The shadows of tribal names and stories are the ventures of landscapes, even in the distance of translation. Tribal imagination, experience, and remembrance, are the real landscapes in the literature of this nation; discoveries and dominance are silence.

N. Scott Momaday, the poet and novelist, reached to the remembrance of his childhood at Jemez, New Mexico. "I existed in that landscape," he wrote in his memoir, *The Names*, "and then my existence was indivisible with it. I placed my shadow there in the hills, my voice in the wind that ran there, in those old mornings and afternoons, and evenings. It may be that the old people there watch for me in the streets; it may be so." That place is so with his memories.

"The language of white thought has had to create the boundaries of its existence and to determine what will not be allowed inside," wrote Aldon Lynn Nielsen in *Reading Race*. "The signifier of whiteness continues to rewrite itself as a discourse into our institutions, including our literature, and we, as racial subject, continue to read it, to recognize it, to privilege it, and to enjoy its power."

The attention to manifest manners and the romance of the land would annihilate tribal names, languages, oral stories, and natural reason. Larzer Ziff argued that literary "annihilation, in which the representation offers itself as the only aspect of the represented that is still extant, is not, of course, physical extermination." However, in "order to conquer the savage one had to outdo him in savagery," and "the wild man within was purged even as the wild man without was exterminated."

The word Indian, and most other tribal names, are simulations in the literature of dominance. Chippewa, for instance, is defined as *otchipwe*, and the invented word Indian is defined as *anishinabe* in *A Dictionary of the Otchipwe Language* by Bishop Baraga. This first dictionary of the language published more than a century ago defined *anishinabe* as a man, woman, child, of the *anishinabe* tribe, but the simulated names, not the names in tribal languages, were sustained by manifest manners in literature.

Cognation and certain loan words can be traced to the earliest use in the literature of dominance. *Canoe*, for instance, was "picked up from the Indians in the West Indies by Columbus's sailors," observed H. L. Mencken in *The American Language*. "It was taken without change into Spanish where it remains as *canoa* to this day." *Maize* is another loan word that came into Spanish and then English from the West Indies. The word *Indian*, however, is a colonial enactment, not a loan word, and the dominance is sustained by the simulation that has superseded the real tribal names.

The Indian was an occidental invention that became a bankable simulation; the word has no referent in tribal languages or cultures. The postindian is the absence of the invention, and the end of representation in literature; the closure of that evasive melancholy of dominance. Manifest manners are the simulations of bourgeois decadence and melancholy.

The postindian warrior is the simulation of survivance in new stories. Indians, and other simulations, are the absence of tribal intimation; the mere mention of blunders in navigation undermines the significance of discoveries and the melancholy of dominance. The contrivance of names, however, endures in the monologues of manifest manners and literature of dominance. The postindian warriors ensnare the contrivances with their own simulations of survivance.

Russell Means, for instance, launched a new simulation of the name. There is "some confusion about the word *Indian*, a mistaken belief that it refers somehow to the country, India," he wrote in

Mother Jones. "Columbus called the tribal people he met 'Indio,' from the Italian *in dio*, meaning 'in God.'"

The postindian warriors bear their own simulations and revisions to contend with manifest manners, the "authentic" summaries of ethnology, and the curse of racialism and modernism in the ruins of representation. The wild incursions of the warriors of survivance undermine the simulations of the unreal in the literature of dominance.

Postindian simulations arise from the silence of heard stories, or the imagination of oral literature in translation, not the absence of the real in simulated realities; the critical distinction is that postindian warriors create a new tribal presence in stories. The simulations of manifest manners are dominance, the scriptures of a civilization in paradise. The counteractions of postindian warriors are the simulations of survivance.

The postindian encounters with manifest manners and the simulations of the other are established in names and literature. This is a continuous turn in tribal narratives, the oral stories are dominated by those narratives that are translated, published, and read at unnamed distances. Stories that arise in silence are the sources of a tribal presence. The simulations of dominance and absence of the other are the concern of manifest manners. The simulations of survivance are heard and read stories that mediate and undermine the literature of dominance.

The names of the postindian warriors are new, but their encounters are consistent with the warriors who tread the manifest manners of past missions in tribal communities. The warriors of simulations, then and now, uncover the absence of the real and undermine the comparative poses of tribal traditions.

The warrior modes and postindian interpretations, in this instance, at the closure of the colonial inventions of the tribes in literature; the warriors, then and now, observe postmodern situations, theories of simulation, deconstruction, postindian encounters, silence, remembrance, and other themes of survivance that would trace the inventions of tribal cultures by missionaries and ethnologists to the truancies and cruelties of a melancholy civilization.

The postindian warriors and the missionaries of manifest manners are both responsible for simulations; even that resemblance is a simulation that ends in silence, or the presence of an original referent to tribal survivance. The warriors of simulation are entitled to tease the absence of remembrance in the ruins of representation, and in the tribal performance of heard stories. Simulations in oral stories arise from silence not inscriptions. The causal narratives of missionaries and ethnologists are terminal simulations of dominance, not survivance.

"But the matter is more complicated, since to simulate is not simply to feign," continued Jean Baudrillard in *Simulacra and Simulations*. "Someone who feigns an illness can simply go to bed and make believe he is ill. Someone who simulates an illness produces in himself some of the symptoms." Hence, "feigning or dissimulating leaves the realty principle intact: the difference is always clear, it is only masked; whereas simulation threatens the difference between 'true' and 'false,' between 'real' and 'imaginary.' Since the simulator produces 'true' symptoms, is he ill or not?"

Jamake Highwater simulated his tribal descent, to be sure, and with such assurance that others feigned their own identities in his presence. Jack Anderson, the investigative columnist, reported that Highwater "fabricated much of the background that made him famous." He was more answerable as a simulation than others were to their own real crossblood identities.

How are we to understand the common attributions of tribal descent in the simulations of postindian identities? Some postindian warriors feign the sources of their own crossblood identities, the masks of a real tribal presence. Others, the wannabes, posers, and the missionaries of manifest manners, would threaten the remembrance of tribal identities with their surveillance and terminal simulations; the scriptures of dominance are the absence of tribal realities not the sources of a presence. The simulations of manifest manners have never been the masks of civilization or even the historical ironies of tribal cultures.

The Indian is the simulation of the absence, an unreal name; however, the misnomer has a curious sense of legal standing. Some of the definitions are ethnological, racial, literary, and juristic sanctions. "To be considered an Indian for federal purposes, an individual must have some Indian blood," wrote Stephen Pevar in *The Rights of Indian Tribes*. "Some federal laws define an Indian as anyone of Indian descent, while other laws require one-fourth or one-half Indian blood in order to be considered as an Indian for purposes of those laws. Still other federal laws define Indian as anyone who has been accepted as a member of a 'federally recognized' Indian tribe." Clearly, the simulations of tribal names, the absence of a presence in a mere tribal misnomer, cannot be sustained by legislation or legal maneuvers.

Postindian autobiographies, the averments of tribal descent, and the assertions of crossblood identities, are simulations in literature; that names, nicknames, and the shadows of ancestors are stories is an invitation to new theories of tribal interpretation.

The sources of natural reason and tribal consciousness are doubt and wonder, not nostalgia or liberal melancholy for the lost wilderness; comic not tragic, because melancholy is cultural boredom, and the tragic is causal, the closure of natural reason. The shimmers of imagination are reason and the simulations are survivance, not dominance; an aesthetic restoration of trickster hermeneutics, the stories of liberation and survivance without the dominance of closure. Tribal consciousness is wonder, chance, coincidence, not the revisions of a pedate paradise; even so, for curious reasons some would hear confessions and the conversions of criminals as the evidence of a new tribal awareness.

Trickster hermeneutics is the interpretation of simulations in the literature of survivance, the ironies of descent and racialism, transmutation, third gender, and themes of transformation in oral tribal stories and written narratives. Trickster stories arise in silence, not scriptures, and are the *holotropes* of imagination; the manifold turns of scenes, the brush of natural reason, characters that liberate the mind and never reach a closure in stories. Trickster stories are the postindian simulations of tribal survivance.

The trickster is reason and mediation in stories, the original translator of tribal encounters; the name is an intimation of transformation, men to women, animals to birds, and more than mere causal representation in names. Tricksters are the translation of creation; the trickster creates the tribe in stories, and pronounces the moment of remembrance as the trace of liberation. The animals laughed, birds cried, and there were worried hearts over the everlasting humor that would liberate the human mind in trickster stories. Trickster stories are the translation of liberation, and the shimmer of imagination is the liberation of the last trickster stories.

Trickster hermeneutics is access to trickster stories, and the shimmer of a tribal presence in simulations; this new course of tribal interpretation arises from the postindian turns in literature, the reach of tribal shadows, postmodern conditions of translation, the traces of deconstruction, and the theories of representation and simulation. Trickster hermeneutics is survivance, not closure, and the discernment of tragic wisdom in tribal experiences. The tribes bear the simulations of pathos and the tragic without the wisdom of chance and natural miseries of the seasons. Simulation of the tragic has been sustained by the literature of dominance. Natural reason teases the sense that nature is precarious; however, the realities of chance, fate, and tragic wisdom were denied in the literature of dominance.

"Some say that tragedy teaches us the power of chance, of the force of contingency in determining whether the virtuous thrive," wrote Amélie Oksenberg Rorty in *Essays on Aristotle's Poetics*. "While tragedy does indeed focus on what can go wrong in the actions of the best of men, its ethical lessons are not primarily about the place of accident and fortune in the unfolding of a human life." She observed that many "tragedies represent a tale with which the audience is likely to be familiar." The tragic tribal tales, in this sense, are simulations for an audience familiar with manifest manners and the literature of dominance. Decidedly, the stories that turn the tribes tragic are not their own stories.

Manifest manners are scriptural simulations, the causal narratives of racialism, the denial of tragic wisdom, and the cultural leases of objectivism; otherwise, the mere mention of the transitive other, the antiselves in the absence of remembrance, would end in silence. The postindian warriors hear stories that arise in natural silence. Listen, oral stories are the best performance of simulations, because the reference is in the performance.

Performance and human silence are strategies of survivance. Nature is a simulation without silence. The presence of human silence and death have no simulations. The absence and the presence of death are mortal performances. "Death actually discloses the imposture of reality, not only in that the absence of duration gives the lie to it, but above all because death is the great affirmer," wrote Georges Bataille in *Theory of Religion*. "But death suddenly shows that the real society was lying. Then it is not the loss of the thing, of the useful member, that is taken into consideration. What the real society has lost is not a member but rather its truth."

Native American Indians have endured the lies and wicked burdens of discoveries, the puritanical destinies of monotheism, manifest manners, and the simulated realities of dominance, with silence, traces of natural reason, trickster hermeneutics, the interpretation of tribal figurations, and the solace of heard stories.

The various translations, interpretations, and representations of the absence of tribal realities have been posed as the verities of certain cultural traditions. Moreover, the closure of heard stories in favor of scriptural simulations as authentic representations denied a common brush with the shimmer of humor, the sources of tribal visions, and tragic wisdom; tribal imagination and creation stories were obscured without remorse in national histories and the literature of dominance.

"One of the greatest paradoxes of contemporary culture is that at a time when the image reigns supreme the very notion of a creative human imagination seems under mounting threat," wrote Richard Kearney in *The Wake of Imagination.* "The imminent demise of imagination is clearly a postmodern obsession. Postmodernism undermines the modernist belief in the image as an *authentic* expression."

In other words, the postindian warriors of postmodern simulations would undermine and surmount, with imagination and the performance of new stories, the manifest manners of scriptural simulations and "authentic" representations of the tribes in the literature of dominance.

Russell Means, for instance, posed with other radical leaders of the American Indian Movement at the occupation of Wounded Knee and landed in motion pictures and a laudable postindian simulation, a studio production of a silk screen portrait by Andy Warhol.

"How about the *American Indian* series?" asked Patrick Smith in *Warhol: Conversations about the Artist.* "Was that any particular Indian?"

"Yeah. That was Russell Means," said Ronnie Cultrone who was, at the time, a studio production assistant to Andy Warhol. "He was involved with the Wounded Knee Massacre, which I don't really know too much about, to tell you the truth. But I think he's still in court. I don't know. Something like that." Indeed, the studio production is a simulation in three dimensions, the absence, presence, and portrait of the militant leader of the American Indian Movement.

This portrait is not an Indian.

René Magritte inscribed "*Ceci n'est pas une pipe*, This is not a pipe," across his painting of an obvious pipe. This ambiguous critique "exemplifies the penetration of discourse into the form of things; it reveals discourse's ambiguous power to deny and to redouble," wrote Michel Foucault in *This Is Not a Pipe*.

Magritte said, "Sometimes the name of an object takes the place of an image. A word can take the place of an object in reality. An image can take the place of a word in a proposition."

Russell Means, with all that, is not a portrait of an Indian. The portrait of an Indian, the silk screen acrylic image of the *American Indian* by Andy Warhol, is denied by the assertion, "This is not an Indian." The portraiture is the absence; the assertion is an ambiguous discourse on simulations and the sources of tribal identities.

"To tell the truth, art must always be forgery—a perfect counterfeit," asserted Arthur Kroker in *The Possessed Individual*, "This is the secret of its fatal seduction, and the promise of its aesthetic destiny. Here, art only succeeds to the extent that it compels the disappearing order of the real," the real as sex, subject, and space, "to vanish into a virtual world of perspectival simulacra. Art, then as an enchanted simulation of trompe l'oeil." Means is not a portrait, he is the postindian warrior of simulations; the absence, not the presence in the simulation.

Means had been on trial in federal court in connection with an armed occupation, but he was not "involved with the Wounded Knee Massacre" or other misnomers and conspiracies. There were no treacheries in the tribal simulations of radical liberation. Federal prosecutors accused him, no doubt, of wild violations of manifest manners on a reservation of his choice. The warrior of simulations told the federal jurors that "because all living things come from one mother, our Mother Earth . . . we have to treat one another with the same respect and reverence that we would our own blood relatives. But the important thing in our philosophy is that we believe we're the weakest things on earth, that the two-legged is the weakest thing on earth because we have no direction."

Means has never been a simulation of weakness; he must have more than two dimensions because he never seems to be without some direction. Without a doubt he is one of the most esteemed postindian warriors of simulations in tribal stories and histories. Honored, accused, and humored, he is a wise warrior of survivance.

Means was a candidate for president of the Oglala Sioux Tribal Council and he aspired, with Larry Flynt, the hustler of *Hustler*, to become the president of the United States. Means lost both elections, but his simulations were more heartened as Chingachgook in the film *The Last of the Mohicans*. He has countered manifest manners and the simulations of dominance in education, politics, and motion pictures, and he has created new stories about tribal rights, philosophies, and traditions.

"I have been asked whether my decision to act in *The Last of the Mohicans* means that I've abandoned my role as an activist," he said in *Entertainment Weekly*. "On the contrary, I see film as an extension of the path I've been on for the past 25 years—another avenue to eliminating racism."

Means has been married four times. "This is my last chance to experience real Indian fatherhood," he said in *People*. "The family, that's what Indians, what Chingachgook, is all about."

Means was arrested several years ago by Navajo police officers when "he attempted to make a citizen's arrest of the Bureau of Indian Affairs area director," James Stevens, at the tribal government center in Window Rock. He accused the director of "interfering in Navajo political matters," reported the *Independent* in Gallup, New Mexico.

"I'm scared because I want to be free and we're not going to be free until you are free," he said last year at the City Club of Cleveland. He created a counter word culture in his lecture and revealed his nerve as a warrior of new simulations.

"Abolish the Bureau of Indian Affairs," he announced. "Get rid of the Bureau, we have a right to fail." Means has pursued an incongruous theme and simulation of abolition in other situations. As a candidate for tribal president he said he would establish prohibition on the reservation and "crime would disappear." He lost the election.

The postindian warrior of simulations has announced in the past two decades scores of abolitions and new identities. "My culture, the Lakota culture, has an oral tradition, so I ordinarily reject writing," *someone* wrote in *Mother Jones*. "So what you read here is not what I've written. It's what I've said and someone else has written down. I will allow this because it seems that the only way to communicate with the white world is through the dead, dry leaves of a book." Means said, "We don't want power over white institutions; we want white institutions to disappear. *That's* revolution."

Means told Alex Demyanenko in the *LA Village View* that "the name game is played out every day" and "racism just rolls off the tongue so easily in this country when it comes to us. They call us tribes. We're not tribes. We're nations. We made treaties. We're the reason why this country has a representative government *supposedly*, allegedly to champion individual rights."

The postindian warrior of cinematic simulations censures the obvious, interracial marriages, and unmans his own imagination with racialism. "The fox doesn't make it with the eagle. The doves don't make it with pigeons. Scorpions don't make it with black widows. It's natural law. It's common sense," he said. Nonsense, and his taboos and proscriptions misconstrue the natural pleasure of trickster figuration and the tribal creation stories. The warriors who turn simulations into prohibitions, rather than liberation and survivance, are themselves the treacherous taboos of dominance.

Means visited the Miskito Indians of Nicaragua and was touched by the unity he observed in their communities. "They never pointed a finger at us and said, 'if you hadn't come, we wouldn't be bombed,'" reported the *Navajo Times*. "They were so noble and Indian, that they came to us very humble and begged our forgiveness for being in danger."

This portrait is not an Indian.

Paula Gunn Allen, the most honored postindian warrior of simulations in literature, pronounced in *The Sacred Hoop* that "the major difference between most activist movements and tribal societies is that for millennia American Indians have based their social systems, however diverse, on ritual, spirit-centered, woman-focused worldviews." Moreover, she wrote, "American Indian thought is essentially mystical and psychic in nature."

Allen conceived the word "cosmogyny" in *Grandmothers of the Light: A Medicine Woman's Sourcebook*. Cosmogynies are simulations that uncover "a spiritual system that is arranged in harmony with gynocratic values." The stories in this sourcebook "connect us to the universe of medicine," she announced in the preface. "Gynocentric communities tend to value peace, tolerance, sharing, relationship, balance, harmony, and just distribution of goods."

The crystal skull, a spectacular carving of a head in clear rock crystal is the source of incredible postindian medicine stories. Allen avowed that she "channeled information" from the "immortal" remains of the skull, a "being" with a "powerful and beautiful presence." She named the carved rock head Crystal Woman.

The spiritual simulations in crystal were the cause of creation and medicine stories. Allen "channeled" to understand that Crystal Woman was a "priestess, a shaman, a medicine woman." She came before "the human beings, before the five-fingered beings."

Allen revealed that two men found the skull in Belize. "In the fullness of time, they found the place where the skull had come to light, and after a time they discovered its present home. They made their way far to the north, to the crisp, suburban home of Sun Woman, Daughter of Light. . . . It is said that the Mother of All and Everything, the Grandmother of the Sun and the Dawn, will return to her children and with her will come harmony, peace, and the healing of the world." Everything must be more obscure on the channel, the encounter with an absence, otherwise these names would lose their postindian significance.

The crystal skull was purchased from "Tiffany of New York in the late 1890s" and may have "originally been brought from Mexico by a Spanish officer," wrote Mark Jones, the editor of *Fake? The Art of Deception.* "Past speculation has suggested that the skull is in fact of Far Eastern origin, but at the time of its entry into the collections of the British Museum it had generally come to be accepted as being from pre-Hispanic Mexico." The skull appears to be Aztec. When it was last examined, however, "the conclusion was that some of the incised lines forming the teeth seemed more likely to have been cut with a jeweler's wheel than to have been produced by the techniques available to Aztec lapidaries." The skull could have been created by a tribal artist for a church or cathedral. "Other speculations as to the origins and possible use of the crystal skull are legion. The question remains open."

Crystal Woman and the crystal skull have more than one simulation in common with the medicine woman, Agnes Whistling Elk, created by Lynn Andrews. The authors, their simulations, crystal manners, and arcane stories arouse millions of readers, most of them women who are reassured once more that literature is "authentic," the real, a source of presence, "gynocratic" medicine, and simulations of utopian peace.

"When I first met Agnes, I asked her if she thought it was strange for someone from Beverly Hills to be sitting in her quiet cabin in Manitoba asking for help," wrote Lynn Andrews in *Flight of the Seventh Moon*. She describes how "Agnes initiated me into my womanliness and selfhood" with visions and ceremonies.

"No, it is not surprising that you are here. Many omens have spoken of your coming, and I would be surprised if it were any other way. You know that enlightenment is arrived at in a different way for a woman than for a man," reported Andrews.

"I asked Agnes if she taught men the same as woman. She laughed and said I should discover that answer for myself. 'Teach the next ten men you meet how to have a baby.'"

Agnes "said that it had been told to her in a prophecy that I was to become a warrioress of the rainbow of black, white, red, and yellow peoples, and that one day I would become a bridge between the two distinct worlds of the primal mind and the white consciousness," Andrews wrote in *Jaguar Woman*.

Andrews pursues racialism and rainbows, to be sure, but she has never been a warrior of postindian survivance; she is the absence of a warrior, the headmost simulator of manifest manners and ersatz spiritualism in the literature of dominance.

The postindian warriors and posers are not the new shaman healers of the unreal. Simulations and the absence of the real are curative by chance; likewise, to hover over the traces of the presence in literature is not an ecstatic vision. The turns of postindian remembrance are a rush on natural reason. Some simulations are survivance, but postindian warriors are wounded by the real. The warriors of simulations are worried more by the real than other enemies of reference. Simulations are the substitutes of the real, and those who pose with the absence of the real must fear the rush of the real in their stories.

The missionaries of manifest manners have flourished for centuries with such ease in politics, education, communications, and literature. The simulated realities of tribal cultures, the most unsure representations, have informed presidents, journalists, college teachers, and publishers for several centuries.

President Ronald Reagan, for instance, told university students on his official visit to Moscow, "Maybe we made a mistake in trying to maintain Indian cultures. Maybe we should not have humored them in wanting to stay in that kind of primitive lifestyle."

William Least Heat-Moon, the author of *Blue Highways* and *PrairyErth*, is another cause of manifest manners and simulations in the literature of dominance. "If there really are such things as American longings," he wrote in a foreword to the new edition of *Old Indian Trails* by Walter McClintock, "surely one of them must be the wish to put aside our modernity with all its emptiness and complex disturbances and to go live as the Indians did before the Europeans descended here. Perhaps even better, to join a tribe with old ways and discover whether life with people only slightly beyond a stone-age culture is sweeter than ours, to learn whether tribal Americans truly built their lives around a harmony and balance between humankind and the rest of nature."

Heat-Moon assumes a surname and embraces pronouns that would undermine his own intended identities as a postindian author. He simulates the presence of the tribal other as "slightly beyond a stone-age culture" and denies an obvious tribal attribution with the phrase, "sweeter than ours." In *PrairyErth* he creates a county with manifest manners and no more than a romantic trace of native tribal cultures. The tribes were reduced to curious silhouettes, not the stories of survivance. Alas, he is amused by a character named Venerable Tashmoo, "a Canadian, with some Ojibway blood." He said, "If Tecumseh had owned a Chevy, he'd never have said selling a county was like trying to sell air or the clouds."

Charles A. Lindbergh, the aviator and adventurer, wrote in his lucid *Autobiography of Values* that his grandfather, who had emigrated from Sweden and settled in Minnesota, "started the community's first school in his farm granary." The school, of course, is an admirable remembrance, but the land, the stolen land and removal of tribal families to reservations, was a mere mention in the literature of dominance. "Children of those days lived in constant fear of Indians, though the Chippewa were friendly and even if, as grownups told them quite truthfully, there was no longer any danger from the Sioux. Now and then, when parents were out of hearing, boys would hide in bushes and whoop like savages to frighten sisters and their friends." The manifest manners were the tired simulations of savagism, at least, that his parents would not hear but in the pleasure of his memories.

"When the real is no longer what it used to be, nostalgia assumes its full meaning," wrote Baudrillard in *Simulacra and Simulations*. "There is a proliferation of myths of origin and signs of reality; of second-hand truth, objectivity and authenticity." Nostalgia, and the melancholia of dominance, are common sources of simulations in manifest manners; mother earth and the shamans of the other are summoned to surrender their peace and harmonies in spiritual movements.

Ed McGaa, the postindian warrior of simulations and sun dance ceremonies, nominated a new rainbow tribe to counter savagism and manifest manners. "The red people had no need to consider migration from their nature-based system," he wrote in *Rainbow Tribe*. "Their land was kept pure and clean. It was still very productive and was not overpopulated." He claims that such "treasures" as "harmonious sociology, unselfish leadership, warm family kinship, and honest justice" proliferated in traditional tribal cultures. The simulations of his rainbow tribe are treacherous, in one sense, because nostalgia is the absence of the real, not the presence of imagination and the wild seasons of peace. The rainbow tribe is a diversion, it would seem, a simulation marooned in the romance of the noble savage and the unattainable salvation of absolute boredom and melancholy.

"We invent the real in the hope of seeing it unfold as a great ruse," wrote Baudrillard in *Fatal Strategies*. People "seek a fatal diversion." No "matter how boring, the important thing is to increase boredom; such an increase is salvation, it is ecstasy."

McGaa, however, had not invented the salvation of the rainbow tribe when he was a law student at the University of South Dakota. Then he lectured in public schools and on reservations about his missions as a combat fighter pilot in Vietnam.

"I remember a touching scene when I was in law school and flying helicopters" for the Marine Corps Reserves. "We circled to land and were met formally by a marching contingent of Sioux warriors" on the Standing Rock Reservation. "We were told to march at the head of the contingent" into the packed gymnasium. "I told the excited crowd that it was an honor to return to a land of tribal people who appreciated the sacrifice of their warriors. I told them how they had salved my spirit with their honoring medicine and how this medicine was deeply appreciated by all the living who returned" from Vietnam.

"Many Sioux warriors from this Hunkpapa and Minnecoujou Sioux reservation had been killed," continued McGaa. "A flag for each departed warrior was raised on its own sapling staff, and the Sioux anthem and our national anthem were played. . . . In the background, draped from two taller poles, the American flag and a tribal flag waved. It was an extremely moving scene cast upon the computer of life."

McGaa, at that time, was the secret witness for the prosecution in a commutation hearing on a capital punishment case before the South Dakota Board of Pardons and Paroles. Thomas White Hawk had been sentenced to death for a brutal murder, and the defense counsel had enlisted more than a hundred tribal witnesses to testify against capital punishment. The combat aviator testified that he was a second-year law student and "half Indian."

"Have you formed an opinion as to the commutation of White Hawk's sentence?" asked the prosecutor, Charles Wolsky.

"Yes, I have formed an opinion," he testified at the commutation hearing. "Well, the old-time Indian had three main methods of punishment. We had outright capital punishment. We had banishment or we had forgiveness. . . . banishment was usually when you did something to your people. They would banish you from the tribe," he explained, and compared banishment to capital punishment. "The outright death penalty was when the tribe would kill you for a real grave serious crime where you brought tremendous disgrace and despair upon your people."

McGaa, on a mission of manifest manners, was the sole witness for the prosecution. Later, outside the hearing room, he was nervous and troubled. He looked back and asked, "Who was that old man in there?" Charles White Hawk, uncle of the condemned murderer, attended the hearing; he sat with his arms folded over his chest and stared at the witness when he testified.

"White Hawk, White Hawk," shouted McGaa, "that old man is a medicine man and he was doing his power on me in there." Indeed, the tribal medicine of survivance, and the man who would simulate a rainbow tribe had lost the seasons.

Governor Frank Farrar announced that he had reviewed the case of Thomas White Hawk and, on 24 October 1969, "commuted his sentence of death in the electric chair to a sentence of life imprisonment for so long as he shall live with the personal request to future Boards of Pardons and Paroles that all petitions for further commutation of the sentence" be denied.

"The Indian is a true child of the forest and the desert," wrote Francis Parkman in *The Conspiracy of Pontiac.* "His haughty mind is imbued with the spirit of the wilderness, and the light of civilization falls on him with a blighting power."

Parkman, one of the masters of manifest manners and the simulations of savagism, considered civilization a blight to the other; such adversities as alcohol, uncouth missionaries, wicked debaucheries, avarice, fraud, corruption, violence, and colonial melancholy, in the occupation of the new nation, were the overload, not the light of civilization. The tribes must have perceived the heart of darkness, not the light of blight, in manifest manners and the cruelties of civilization.

"The shadows of his wilderness home, and the darker mantle of his own inscrutable reserve, have made the Indian warrior a wonder and mystery," continued Parkman. His romantic and sinister simulations that the "generous traits are overcast" by "sleepless distrust" and suspicions of "treachery in others," are the histories and literature of dominance.

"Ambition, revenge, envy, jealousy, are his ruling passions; and his cold temperament is little exposed to those effeminate vices which are the bane of milder races. With him revenge is an overpowering instinct; nay, more, it is a point of honor and a duty."

Parkman mentions the unscrupulous trade in diluted and poisonous alcoholic beverages in *The Old Régime in Canada*. "The drunken Indian with weapons within reach, was very dangerous, and all prudent persons kept out of his way. This greatly pleased him; for, seeing everybody run before him, he fancied himself a great chief, and howled and swung his tomahawk with redoubled fury. If, as often happened, he maimed or murdered some wretch not nimble enough to escape, his countrymen absolved him from all guilt, and blamed only the brandy. . . . In the eyes of the missionaries, brandy was a fiend with all crimes and miseries in his train; and, in fact, nothing earthly could better deserve the epithet infernal than an Indian town in the height of a drunken debauch."

Evelyn Waugh observed the tribes with an obverse curse of racialism and manifest manners, but with an ironic touch, that the tribes were similar, in certain respects, to the English. "The Indians, I learned later, are a solitary people and it takes many hours' heavy drinking to arouse any social interests in them," he wrote in *Ninety-two Days: The Account of a Tropical Journey Through British Guiana and Part of Brazil*. "In fact the more I saw of Indians the greater I was struck by their similarity to the English. They like living with their own families at great distances from their neighbours; they regard strangers with suspicion and despair; they are improgressive and unambitious, fond of pets, hunting and fishing; they are undemonstrative in love, unwarlike, morbidly modest; their chief aim seems to be on all occasions to render themselves inconspicuous; in all points, except their love of strong drink and perhaps their improvidence, the direct opposite of the negro."

Native American Indians bear the burdens of a nation cursed with the manifest manners of alcoholism. Once thought to be nutritious, alcohol has been the earnest measure of temperance, and the source of enormous excise revenues from the sale of beverage alcohol.

Alcohol has "crossed regional, sexual, racial, and class lines," asserted William Rorabaugh in *The Alcoholic Republic*. Manifest manners, however, have never understated the racialism of alcohol, or the savage simulations that the tribal other had the real burden, a genetic weakness to alcohol and civilization. Indians are the wild alcoholics in the literature of dominance.

"Americans drank at home and abroad, alone and together, at work and at play, in fun and in earnest," wrote Rorabaugh. The early nineteenth century was a "great alcoholic binge." Americans drank over time, fashion, and their economic miseries, and the tribes became the simulated measure of the national curse of alcoholism; the public has been hesitant to discern the real cost of alcoholism, and reluctant to abandon the stereotype of the drunken savage.

"The colonial view of Indian drinking, that red men could not hold their liquor, was in fact the beginning of a long-standing stereotype of the impact of alcohol on the tribes," wrote Mark Lender and James Martin in *Drinking in America*. The colonial settlers simulated the tribes as savages, and "any sign of intemperate behavior served to confirm that image. Some modern anthropologists have termed the so-called Indian drinking problem the 'firewater myth.' " The authors explain that "some tribes learned to drink from the wrong whites: fur traders, explorers, or fishing crews, all of whom drank hard and, frequently, in a fashion not condoned" by missionaries and other colonists.

"Perhaps no stereotype has been so long-lasting and so thoroughly ensconced in our social fabric as that of the 'drunken Indian.' Our federal government gave it official recognition by prohibiting the sale of beverage alcohol to Indian people for over a century," wrote Joseph Westermeyer in " 'The Drunken Indian': Myths and Realities" in the *Psychiatric Annals*.

The premise that prohibition can subdue alcoholism on reservations has never been renounced. Russell Means, for instance, once declared as a candidate for the presidency of the Oglala Sioux Tribal Council that he would establish "customs checkpoints" around the entire reservation, prohibiting the transportation and sale of beverage alcohol in tribal communities. The advocates of prohibition seem to have increased with the incredible rise of tribal casinos, and even more because some casinos have opened liquor bars on the reservation.

Prohibition is neither a cure nor a resolution of the "firewater myth" in the literature of dominance; however, prohibition espoused by postindian warriors is a simulation of survivance. Means would abolish the institution and manifest manners rather than punish the victims of beverage alcohol.

Louise Erdrich, the poet and novelist, has pronounced one of the most extreme prohibitions as a resolution to the menace of alcohol in the lives of women and children. Fetal Alcohol Syndrome, the situation of acute alcohol poisoning on some reservations, "has grown so desperate that a jail internment during pregnancy has been the only answer possible in some cases," she wrote in the foreword to *The Broken Cord* by Michael Dorris. The use of the word "internment" is a curious euphemism for incarceration, and without the patent due process of law in a constitutional democracy.

"If a woman is pregnant and if she is going to drink alcohol, then, in simple language, she should be jailed," asserted Jeaneen Grey Eagle. Dorris interviewed her on the Pine Ridge Reservation. She was then the director of Project Recovery. He wrote that "her words were shocking, antithetical to every self-evident liberal belief I cherished, yet through my automatic silent denial I felt some current of unexpected assent," and then he asked, "What civil liberty overrode the torment of a child?"

Indeed, alcohol is poison, but must tribal women bear once more the moral burdens of manifest manners? Must tribal women bear the burdens for the distribution of beverage alcohol and the excise revenues on the sale of alcohol? The "internment" of poor tribal women would be an autocratic salvation for the moral crimes of a nation.

Native American Indians have endured the envies of the missionaries of manifest manners for five centuries. The Boy Scouts of America, the wild simulations of tribal misnomers used for football teams, automobiles, and other products, Western movies, and the heroic adventures in novels by James Fenimore Cooper, Frederick Manfred, Karl May, and others are but a few examples of the manifold envies that have become manifest manners in the literature of dominance. The shamans of the tribes have been envied by urban spiritualists, military men have envied the courage of the tribes, and now, on some reservations, the outrageous riches from casino operations are envied by untold posers in organized crime and politics.

Frederick Manfred must have envied tribal warriors and the natural lust of the noble savage to create five Western novels in Buckskin

Man Tales. *Scarlet Plume*, the third in the series, is based on the cruelties of traders and government agents that caused the "Sioux Indian Uprising in Minnesota in 1862." Judith Raveling has been abducted in the novel; the romantic tension of savagism and civilization is an invitation to manifest manners and the literature of dominance. Scarlet Plume is "one of the last pure Dakota Indians, untainted by white ways and beliefs, but doomed himself just as his people are," wrote Arthur Huseboe in the foreword to the novel.

"Presently Judith's eye fell on a dusky young woman sitting just across from her in the gate or the horns of the camp. Her name was Squirts Milk and she seemed to be nursing two little ones, twins, at her ample bosom at the same time. This in itself was unusual enough, until Judith noticed that one of the nurslings was abnormally hairy. . . . The hairy one wasn't a baby at all. It was a puppy. The puppy's little eyes were closed in bliss as it suckled at Squirts Milk's soft tan pap," wrote Manfred in *Scarlet Plume*.

"She had always admired Scarlet Plume, had even had a love dream about him. How right she had been about him. Once in the long, long ago he had thrown a dead white swan at her feet to warn her that she must fly to save her neck. And he still wished to save her. Yes. Yes. He was more than just a simple red man. He was a great man. . . . His rich, wide lips were those of a lover, graven upon weathered copper. He was all man. A god among men. He made her think of the old Greek heroes: Achilles and Ajax and Odysseus. She found it difficult to think him a deadly enemy, a Cuthead Sioux."

The envies of the warriors, redoubtable visions, and spiritual ceremonies of the tribes have become simulations in a consumer culture. Silence and death are not enviable simulations, but the envies of manifest manners have ruined the solace of a natural and precarious landscape, and the intimate memories of chance in tribal stories. Once more, the outcome of reservation casinos could be decided by those who were the most envious of the tribal other, the romantic antiselves, and now the riches of the other, and tribal sovereignty. Hannah Arendt argued in *Antisemitism* that the persecution of those who are powerless "may not be a very pleasant spectacle, but it does not spring from human meanness alone. What makes men obey or tolerate real power and, on the other hand, hate people who have wealth without power, is the rational instinct that power has a certain function and is of some general use." The new wealth from casinos has not recast reservations into states of real power with established policies; the power that would not incite the envies of the enemies of tribalism.

"Even exploitation and oppression still make society work and establish some kind of order," continued Arendt. "Only wealth without power or aloofness without a policy are felt to be parasitical, useless, revolting, because such conditions cut" the threads that tie people together. "To be aware of such general rules is important only in order to refute those recommendations of common sense which lead us to believe that violent hatred or sudden rebellion spring necessarily from great power and great abuses. . . ."

The simulations of tribal power and the envies of casino riches are the absence of power, and the conditions of antisemitism could, in this instance, be compared to the latent violence of antitribalism. The intractable situations of hatred, abuse, and extreme racialism could be mediated, in a curious manner, by the literature of dominance. Arendt pointed out that "neither oppression nor exploitation as such is ever the main cause for resentment; wealth without visible function is much more intolerable because nobody can understand why it should be tolerated."

The obvious riches of tribal casinos and the arrogance of wealth on some reservations that were otherwise simulated as extreme environments of destitution, alcoholism, and family destruction are the conditions that would invite wicked envies and antitribalism. The tension of selected wealth without power, the impoverishment on most reservations, and the constant pursuit of entitlements from the federal government must rouse the envious and the enemies of tribal sovereignty.

"The explosion of Indian gambling into a billion-dollar industry also has created a legal backlash from state authorities," wrote Jonathan Littman in an essay on Indian gaming in the *California Lawyer*. "States with existing gambling prohibitions are challenging the federal government's right to impose reservation gaming within their borders. The Indian tribes won the early rounds, but states have devised a new strategy based on their own constitutional sovereignty rights."

The Indian Gaming Regulatory Act recognized that the tribes have the "exclusive right to regulate gaming" on reservations if the activity is not prohibited by either federal or state laws. The new law established three classes of gaming: the first, traditional tribal games; the second, games such as bingo, lotto, and pulltabs; the third, and most controversial of the three classes, includes lotteries, slot machines, blackjack, pari-mutuel betting, and other casino games.

"For the past decade, a fight has been raging over what forms of gambling, if any, American Indians should be allowed to have on their own reservations," wrote I. Nelson Rose in *Indian Gaming and the Law*. "Ever since the Seminole Tribe in Florida won the right in 1979 to run high-stakes bingo games free from government control, the controversy has been fought in legislatures, in press, and cases going all the way to the United States Supreme Court." The Indian Gaming Regulatory Act of 1988 "eliminates the anomalous situation where private individuals have been operating gambling games without control solely because they are on Indian land."

Tribal leaders have maintained that casinos are located on sovereign tribal land, outside of state jurisdiction. Nonetheless, federal agents raided casinos and seized machines to enforce the gaming laws on five reservations in Arizona. The seizure was blocked by tribal people on one reservation until the governor negotiated a temporary agreement with the tribes that operated casinos in the state.

The Foxwoods Casino in Connecticut reached an agreement with the governor to permit slot machines in accordance with class three of the new gaming law. Governor Lowell Weicker, who had opposed casinos in the state, agreed to slot machines with the Mashantucket Pequot Indians. The "tribe in turn agreed to contribute at least $100 million a year in gambling profits to a fund to aid troubled cities and towns," reported the *New York Times*.

Garrison Keillor reigns as the inscrutable monarch of manifest manners at the Chatterbox Café and the Pretty Good Grocery. "We sat in the weeds, decked out in commando wear," he wrote in *Lake Wobegon Days*, "and we looked down the slope to the roofs of town, which sometimes were German landing boats pulled up on the beach, and other times were houses of despicable white settlers who had violated the Sacred Hunting Ground of us Chippewa. We sent volleys of flaming arrows down on them and burned them to the ground many times."

Keillor explained with the sardonicism of manifest manners that the name "Lake Wobegon" is not woebegone. "To scholars of the Ojibway tongue, 'Wobegon' or 'Wa-be-gan-tan-han' means 'the place where [we] waited all day in the rain,' but some translated the word as simply 'patience' and it was used by the *Star* in that sense." The simulation of woebegone is the absence of patience in the ruins of representation.

The Anishinaabe told wild stories about the bleached "clay monsters," or the "despicable white settlers" at Lake Wobegon, Minnesota. The name "Wobegon" comes from two Anishinaabe tribal words: the first, *wabawan*, means the "white of the egg," and the second, *wabigan*, means "clay." One of the settlers heard these survivance stories and names and she combined the words to mean the "clay monsters."

The Native American Indian "has much Wild Man in him, and it comes out in love of ordinary things," wrote Robert Bly in *Iron John*. "Lame Deer mentions over and over in his autobiography that the Indian experiences the divine in a bit of animal hide, in mist or steam, and in ordinary events of the day. A Chippewa wild woman wrote this little poem:

> *Sometimes I go about pitying myself,*
> *And all the time*
> *I am being carried on great winds across the sky."*

Robert Bly, the wild man of manifest manners, has turned an obscure translation of a tribal song into a simulation of a poem; he transvalued the sense of the song story into the silence of a written poem as a measure of dominance in literature. Bly must be the transient poser in tribal literature because this "little poem" was not written by a "Chippewa wild woman." The simulations of manifest manners and dominance are redoubled in other publications. This "little poem," ascribed to Bly, was published by Sierra Club Books in *News of the Universe*, and then as the introduction to the first chapter of *Flight of the Seventh Moon* by Lynn Andrews.

Bly maintains the cause of manifest manners; the insolence of his discoveries and erroneous conversions of tribal literature is elusive but not inconsiderable. He reveals no sources and he does not provide the reader with any mention of the conditions of translation or even an elemental context for the "wild woman" misnomer. Hermeneutics, it would seem, is not in the service of wild men and manifest manners.

Frances Densmore recorded and published the dream song more than eighty years ago in *Chippewa Music*. "Song of the Thunders" was sung by Gagandac at the White Earth Reservation in Minnesota. Densmore published this translation of the dream song:

Sometimes
I go about pitying
Myself
While I am carried by the wind
Across the sky.

Densmore observed that this "song forms an example of the strange personation which characterizes many of the dream songs. In this the singer contemplates the storm mystery of the sky until he feels himself a part of it and sings its song." The dream songs come "in a dream or trance. Many Indian songs are intended to exert a strong mental influence, and dream songs are supposed to have this power in greater degree than any others."

Bly borrowed without attribution the first part of the dream song and changed one sentence in the second part from, "While I am carried by the wind" to his version, "I am being carried on great winds." He reveals no reason for this conversion. The clever sense of time as the singer is carried by the wind, in translation, has been lost to the double indicative of existence on a superlative wind in the conversion.

"The American Indian knew he had gone through a disastrous change in the late nineteenth century," asserted Bly in *American Poetry: Wildness and Domesticity.* The Indian "found he had 'lost his dreams.' The dreams of sacred muskrats or of white stallions with the colors of the four directions painted on their flanks, stopped coming. When he woke up in the morning, his mind was blank." Bly has a blank mind about the presence of the tribes and their stories; he must be *seen* by the tribes in the simulations of his own antiselves. Indeed, and the tribes inured the simulations of silence and wildness of the author.

Bly seems to hound the silence of tribal stories; he could be the wild man of manifest manners in the absence of his own stories. The miseries of a modern man in search of the other, and traces of a wild man in the stories and dream songs of the other, is the melancholia of absence and dominance. "To the magic of the primitive, colonialism fused its own magic, the magic of primitivism," wrote Michael Taussig in *Shamanism, Colonialism, and the Wild Man.* The contradictory figures of the wild and primitive, "less than human and more than human," are the "fetishized antiselves made by civilizing histories."

Iron John "finally settles on the mind as a tangled mop of vivid and cumbrous *nostalgies*," Martin Amis wrote in the *London Review of Books.* "Bly is a poet. He is a big cat, so to speak, and not some chipmunk or beaver from the how-to industry. Then again, maybe Bly is more like a stag or a peacock, contentedly absorbed in the 'display' rituals he so admires."

The first "hermeneutical motion" of translation is "initiative trust, an investment of belief, underwritten by previous experience," wrote George Steiner in *After Babel.* The "demonstrative statement of understanding which is translation, starts with an act of trust."

Native American Indian literatures have endured manifest manners, trust, the aspersions of translation, and conversion for five centuries. Henry Rowe Schoolcraft, one of the most important interpreters of tribal cultures in the early nineteenth century, published his translations of Ojibwa songs and stories in *Algic Researches.* Henry Wadsworth Longfellow was influenced by this material and based his epic poem *Song of Hiawatha*, a memorial to manifest manners, on the translated oral narratives of the Ojibwa who were known as the Chippewa and Anishinaabe. Even tribal dream songs are misused by wild men, the "fetishized antiselves" unleashed in the literature of dominance.

The Song of Hiawatha "sold out of its first printing of 4,000 copies on the day of its publication and completed its first year in print with sales of 38,000," wrote Arnold Krupat in *For Those Who Came After.* "Hiawatha elegiacally counsels his people to abandon the old ways and adapt themselves to the coming of 'civilization,' but he does so in a verse form which only 'civilization' can provide; Longfellow derived *Hiawatha's* trochaic meter from the Finnish epic, *Kalevala.*"

Hiawatha became the sycophant of manifest manners in the literature of dominance.

"Great translators," Steiner argued in *Language and Silence*, "act as a kind of living mirror. They offer to the original not an equivalence, for there can be none, but a vital counterpoise, an echo, faithful yet autonomous, as we find in the dialogue of human love. An act of translation is an act of love. Where it fails, through immodesty or blurred perception, it traduces. Where it succeeds, it incarnates."

Encyclopaedia Britannica sponsored the simulation of tribal manikins as a promotional exhibition in various shopping centers. The manikins were named Black Hawk, Pontiac, Cochise, Massasoit, and the names of other tribal leaders mentioned in the literature of dominance.

The sculptured simulations were stationed in a diorama more than a decade ago to promote one of the most celebrated encyclopaedias, but the unusual feature of the exhibition was that few of the names of the plastic figures were entered in the reference books published by the sponsors of the simulations. The want of manifest manners had excused or abandoned the entries of tribal names in the encyclopaedia of dominance.

"The Indian leaders whose likenesses appear in this exhibition represent every major region of the country and span more than four centuries of history," the editors wrote in the catalogue. "Some were great military leaders who fought valiantly to defend their lands. Others were statesmen, diplomats, scholars and spiritual leaders." The tribal warriors, however, lost their land and the war of manifest manners.

Nine manikins were decorated with feathers and the same number were praised as warriors. Black Hawk, the editors revealed, "established his reputation as a warrior early in life. He wounded an enemy of his tribe at the age of fifteen and took his first scalp the same year."

Three simulations were armed with rifles. Only the manikin named Massasoit was dressed in a breechcloth and carried a short bow.

Otherwise, the Wampanoag tribal leader was associated with the Pilgrims. The other manikins were named Joseph, Cornplanter, Powhatan, Red Cloud, Sequoyah, Tecumseh, Wovoka, and Sacagawea, the one woman in the tribal simulations.

The editors consulted with "scholars in the fields of Indian history, anthropology and ethnology," and pointed out that the simulated biographies in the catalogue were the "product of hundreds of hours of research involving scores of sources of information." Such considerations seem ironic, because most of the tribal names were not entered in the encyclopaedia the sponsors promoted at the exhibitions.

The manikins of Black Hawk and Sequoyah were based on copies of the simulations by the nineteenth century portrait painter Charles Bird King. Sequoyah, the tribal scholar, created a written language in Cherokee. The portrait simulation wears a turban, bears a peace medal around his neck, and smokes a narrow pipe. Sequoyah, the manikin of manifest manners, lost the peace medal and pipe, but the sculpture is decorated with red and white feathers that resemble egret plumes.

Some of the simulations were based on portraits, others were created from historical descriptions, and two manikins were based on photographs. Joseph was dressed in a capote made from a Hudson's Bay Company blanket. Wovoka, the spiritual inspiration of the Ghost Dance religion, was created from several photographs taken by James Mooney. "It seems odd," noted the editors of the catalogue, "that Wovoka is shown dressed in white man's clothes, but this is the costume he typically wore as did many other Indians."

The causal simulations of the tribal other are continuous sources of racial separations in the literature of dominance. "For one person to have tried to separate fact from fiction in every instance would border on the impossible," noted the editors. The manikins as simulations have become the representations of manifest manners. The absence of the tribal real, the unreal simulations, crossed the border of "fact and fiction" and became the real in the promotion of the Encyclopaedia Britannica.

The Wahpeton Indian School in North Dakota was conceived in the assimilation mien of manifest manners. The superintendent of the federal boarding school, a retired military officer, had encouraged some of the better students to tribal dance to the music of the Lord's Prayer.

These momentous dance performances were held for certain visitors in the gymnasium at the school. A tribal child was invited to perform by the superintendent. The child heard the music and danced on the hardwood basketball court. He wore the simulations of a ceremonial headdress made with chicken feathers that had been stained a bright yellow.

The tribal child danced and gestured with his hands, natural turns and circles on the polished court. The gestures were sign language to the words of the Lord's Prayer. The superintendent said the child was one of the best of the Indian sign language dancers.

The child was lonesome and honored to dance, but the invitation was an annihilation of his tribal remembrance. The superintendent was unaware and unashamed, one of the hardhearted missionaries of manifest manners. The observers were sickened by the scene, but endorsed the performance to save that tribal child the humiliation of his favors to manifest manners. The observers participated in one of the most treacherous simulations of the tribal heart, a dance in chicken feathers to please the missionaries. Would we have been wiser to denounce the child at the time, to undermine the simulations of the dance in the presence of the superintendent? We should have told that child then and there our honest reactions to his dance, but we were his audience of solace. How could we be the assassins of his dreams and survivance?

The United States Information Agency sponsored my participation at a special national celebration held near Bonn, Germany. At the same time a liberal foundation in the country had sponsored several tribal dancers to perform at the same cultural ceremonies. Moreover the leader of the tribal dancers was invited, with several others, to participate in a panel discussion.

Udo Phillips, the German television interviewer, demonstrated with his initial comment on tribal alcoholism that racialism and manifest manners are not bound by cultures or nations. Phillips asked the "Chief" if he should be worried about being "scalped." The dancer paused, and then he turned to the interviewer and said, "maybe." The audience was amused and relieved that the tension had ended with courteous humor. Indeed, the manners were untouchable, and secured by the national amenities that would cause envies and racialism.

Phillips pronounced other simulations that revealed the envies of his antitribalism. "Chief," he asked, would you share your money with others on the reservation if you had any? "Chief," are you doing any war dances in the program this afternoon?

The Chief, who never resisted the simulation, introduced the other dancers on the tour and told the audience that one of the dancers would perform the Indian Sign Language Dance to the Lord's Prayer.

This portrait is not an Indian.

Dennis Banks, once the venerable torchbearer of the American Indian Movement, has been recast by the media as a kitschyman of tribal manners and the simulations of capitalism; indeed, he has been one of the postindian worthies of church and state assistance since the late sixties. His stature as a kitschyman of resistance has been authenticated by an ironic letter published by a national syndicated columnist.

"Dear Abby," Banks wrote in response to a reader who had asked about the tribal secrets that please women, and if "Indian men were superior to white men in lovemaking." "For the Indian, 'love' does not begin when the lights go out or when pot or liquor is consumed, and it is not confined to the bedroom or any other hidden place. The way in which the Indian treats his wife throughout his marriage is the key to making him a superior lover.

"While we recognize that the sex act may send man's mind afloat for a few fleeting moments, it is but a minute part of the overall act of love," wrote Banks. "The above code of behavior plus the Indian's respect for women have been passed down from father to son. I have fifteen children and am an Ojibway Indian."

Clyde Bellecourt, one of the many founders of the American Indian Movement, has not been an honorable leader to tribal children; he has earned censure and satirical nomination as the kitschyman of resistance enterprises and industries. A federal grand jury indicted him on nine separate counts of drug distribution, which included one count for conspiracy. Bellecourt was arrested, negotiated a reduced sentence, a guilty plea to one count in the indictment, and served less than two years in federal prison.

The American Indian Movement could be an unusual measure of tribal resistance and the pose of postmodern revolutions. Dennis Banks, for instance, became the kitschyman of reservation capitalism. Russell Means is a postindian movie actor. Bellecourt, on the other hand, has become the kitschyman of liberal bounties, foundation monies, criminal justice, and resistance enterprises in the name of tribal children.

This portrait is not an Indian.

The Office of War Information invited Stephen Vincent Benét to "write a short, interpretive history of the United States for translation into many languages." *America*, one of the common manuals on manifest manners, was published by Holt, Rinehart and Winston at the end of the Second World War.

Benét wrote that when the English landed at Jamestown, "Everything was new and strange to them—the birds, the beasts, the flowers, the Indians, the heart of summer, the very taste of the water in the river. They were awed and dazzled, like children. They died of fever, of starvation, by Indian arrows. Sometimes the Indians would fight them, sometimes be friendly. The settlers never knew which would be which or why."

This portrait is not an Indian.

2

DOUBLE OTHERS

Native American Indian medical doctors are scarce, and for that reason they were once the measure of assimilation and invitational civilization. Tribal healers and shamans were counted as the representations of both demonic and noble savagism; these men and women were studied and romanced as evidence of the other, or the exotic double other, in an "authentic" culture.

These considerations and the transvaluations of cultural values are the means that belie the histories of tribal names and simulations of identities in the literature of dominance.

The postindian shaman is an ecstatic healer in literature and culture, the shadow of tragic wisdom outside the humdrum of time and manners. The shamans bear precarious visions and hear curious stories that are both separations and ministrations to common tribal communities; however, a mere ecstatic vision is not an endorsement because shamans must heal, and the performance of healers must be sanctioned by those who trusted the performance and were healed. Otherwise, the rush to natural reason in the cities could become an avaricious simulation! The double others are the discoveries of the ecstatic separations of one other from the simulations of the other in the representations of an "authentic" tribal culture. Truly, the shamanic double others are the ironic absence of romantic antiselves.

The medical doctor, on the other hand, is a certified simulation bound to time and institutions with traces of tribal culture and dominance; the manifest manners of performance are honored more than ecstatic visions as a healer. The decadence of healers has caused a revolution in the state of simulations; tribal identities have been misconstrued as salvation and other counter sanctions.

Robert Bellah argues in *The Broken Covenant* that the romantic "transvaluation of roles that turns the despised and oppressed into symbols of salvation and rebirth is nothing new in the history of human culture, but when it occurs, it is an indication of new cultural directions, perhaps of a deep cultural revolution."

There are more specious shamans and tribal healers in urban areas than on reservations. In the cities natural reason has been superseded by contrived performances, the simulations that have no shadows of survivance. Medical doctors, the obverse of shamans, the double others in the cities, are weakened as healers in certain tribal communities because they have no stories.

"Caring and curing go hand in hand," wrote Michael Harner in *The Ways of the Shaman*. "Through his heroic journey and efforts, the shaman helps his patients transcend their normal, ordinary definition of reality, including the definition of themselves as ill. The shaman shows his patients that they are not emotionally and spiritually alone in their struggles against illness and death."

Santiago, a tribal leader at the Santo Domingo Pueblo, asked Carl Hammerschlag, the medical doctor in the Indian Health Service, "Do you know how to *dance?*" Hammerschlag humored the patient, "And will you teach me your steps?" Santiago danced at the side of his hospital bed and said, "You must be able to dance if you are to heal people."

Hammerschlag learned to hear stories with natural reason in the course of his practice. "Indian traditions have a strong belief in spirits and the healing presence of sacramental objects," he wrote in *The*

Dancing Healers. "Witchcraft is just the opposite side of that view; it explains the concepts of evil. A concept of evil is necessary to give us a sense of right and wrong, a way of knowing how to treat others. . . . When you believe in witchcraft you also believe that you can get rid of the evil spirit. The task is to find a power greater than that of the witch; it may be a totemic animal, a psychic, a medicine man, a ceremony, surgery, or the confessional."

Charles Alexander Eastman, Ohiyesa, was raised by his paternal grandmother with a tribal name in the traditions of the Santee Sioux. He graduated with distinction from Dartmouth College and the Boston University School of Medicine.

Eastman was one of the first tribal medical doctors determined to serve reservation communities; he became the physician at the Pine Ridge Reservation. A few months later, on December 29, 1890, he treated the few tribal survivors of the Wounded Knee Massacre. The Seventh Cavalry murdered hundreds of ghost dancers and their families at the encampment of Big Foot. Two weeks earlier the tribes mourned the death of Sitting Bull.

Eastman was raised to be a traditional tribal leader, but that natural course would not be honored. His father, Many Lightnings, was imprisoned for three years in connection with the violent conflict of settlers and the Minnesota Sioux in 1862. He would have been hanged but the death sentence was commuted by President Abraham Lincoln. Christianity touched his tribal soul and he chose the name Jacob Eastman.

Charles was about twelve years old when he and his relatives escaped to avoid possible retribution by the military. His sense of a traditional tribal world was never the same after his father was sentenced. His new name, education, and marriage were revolutions in his time; moreover, he was burdened with the remembrance of violence, the separation and conversion of his father, and the horror of the massacre at Wounded Knee.

Eastman and others of his generation, the first to be educated at federal boarding schools, must have been haunted and mortified by the atrocities of the cavalry soldiers. Wounded Knee caused even more posttraumatic burdens than other horrors of war because the stories of the survivors were seldom honored.

The Vietnam Veterans Memorial honors the names of those who lost their lives in the war; their names are shadows in the stone. The names are the remembrance of stories, and the shadows of the names wait to be touched. A Wounded Knee Memorial would honor the names of those who were murdered by the soldiers; the shadows of the ancestors could come to their names in the stone to hear the stories of survivance.

"He arrived one cold and windy day," as the medical doctor at Pine Ridge, South Dakota, wrote H. David Brumble III in *American Indian Autobiography*. "Just one month later he was binding wounds and counting frozen corpses at Wounded Knee."

Eastman reported later that the survivors "objected very strenuously to being treated by army surgeons, alleging as a reason that it was soldiers that had been the cause of their wounds, and they therefore never wanted to see a uniform again."

Brumble rushed to representations in his interpretations; he tied nine lines from *Indian Boyhood* by Eastman into the manifest manners of the vanishing tribal pose. The lines he construed as dismissive of the tribal simulation contain these past-tense phrases: the "Indian was the highest type of pagan and uncivilized man" who possessed a "remarkable mind," but "no longer exists as a natural and free man," and the remnants on the reservation are "a fictional copy of the past."

Brumble strained over these lines; he seemed to be insensitive to the burdens of the manifest manners of discoveries, the presence of antiselves, and the duplicities of assimilation policies, tribal ironies, and counter simulations. He asserted that "*Indian Boyhood* reflects evolutionist ideas," and the autobiography assumes that "the races may be ordered, that some are higher, some lower." Eastman "believed that differing races have different instincts," and "saw himself as an embodiment of Social Darwinist notions about the evolution of the races."

Brumble overstated the assumed influences of evolutionism at the time; his interpretations arise from the distance of literature and are imposed as representations of the intentions of a tribal medical doctor. Brumble traced Eastman with the most controversial notions of evolutionism and determinism. Clearly, the harsh debates over the monogenetic or polygenetic creation and evolution of humans has landed in the interpretation of tribal autobiographies.

"By the end of the first two decades of the nineteenth century, when philanthropy and the churches could show few positive results from their efforts to lift the Indians, doubts were raised about whether they could really be civilized," wrote Robert Bieder in *Science Encounters the Indian*. "Many such critics began to question the monogenetic assumptions, set forth in the Bible, that all mankind shared the same origin. Increasingly they began to explain Indians' recalcitrant nature in terms of polygenism. To polygenists Indians were separately created and were an inferior species of man."

Eastman wrote, "I have never lost my sense of right and justice." He endured the horror of a massacre, the melancholy of racialism, and resisted federal policies on reservations and in government schools. His resistance to manifest manners and dominance was honorable, and more assured, than to tease once more the antiselves of evolutionism.

Frederick Hoxie, director of the D'Arcy McNickle Center for the History of the American Indian, pointed out that Eastman carried out his objective of a "universal quality" and "personal appeal" in *The Soul of the Indian*. "Significantly, his writing avoided identification with a particular tribal tradition, emphasizing instead a generalized and idyllic past." Eastman was an author of the soul, not a servant of the science of racialism at the time; he would counter antiselves and the simulations of savagism.

"Those soldiers had been sent to protect these men, women, and children who had not joined the ghost dancers, but they had shot them down without even a chance to defend themselves," wrote Luther Standing Bear in *My People the Sioux*. "The very people I was following—and getting my people to follow—had no respect for motherhood, old age, or babyhood. Where was all their civilized training?"

Historical mention of that massacre more than a century ago remains scarce. The *American Heritage Dictionary* notes in the geographic entries that Wounded Knee was the "site of the last major battle of the Indian Wars." That a massacre of tribal women and children would become the "last major battle of the Indian Wars" is an instance of manifest manners and the literature of dominance. Elaine Goodale, a poet and teacher from Massachusetts, became the dedicated supervisor of Indian education in the Dakotas. She met the young doctor at Pine Ridge. They were married later that year in New York City. Eastman was troubled by federal authorities and policies on reservations; he tried a private medical practice for a time, and then, after several other positions in federal service, he turned to writing. Later, Charles and Elaine purchased a summer camp in New Hampshire.

"The Indian no more worshipped the Sun than the Christian adores the Cross," he wrote in *The Soul of the Indian*. "The Sun and the Earth, by an obvious parable, holding scarcely more of poetic metaphor than of scientific truth, were in his view the parents of all organic life. From the Sun, as the universal father, proceeds the quickening principle in nature, and in the patient and fruitful womb of our mother, the Earth, are hidden embryos of plants and men."

Eastman endured the treacherous turns and transvaluations of tribal identities, the simulations of ferocious warrior cultures, the myths of savagism and civilization, federal duplicities, assimilation policies, the rise of manifest manners, and the hardhearted literature of dominance. He wrote to teach his readers that the tribes were noble; however, he would be reproached as romantic and censured as an assimilationist. Others honored his simulations of survivance.

"Eastman spent the balance of his long life making his way along the narrow path that bridged his two cultures," wrote Sam Gill in *Mother Earth*. "He was extremely influential and became a major model for the way of resolving the tensions that existed between cultures. . . . He attempted through government service, through lecturing and writing, through participation—often in founding and formative roles—in many organizations such as the YMCA and the Boy Scouts of America, to build bridges of understanding between cultures."

Eastman embraced metaphors over truistic translations to describe tribal religions; he was romantic, but he would disabuse those who pronounce that tribal cultures created the notion of the sun and mother earth as deities. Gill pointed out that his "statement is motivated by the need to counter this view, which he sees is as misplaced as declaring that Christians worship the cross."

Eastman was an outstanding student, and he learned to use metaphors as the simulations of survivance. He celebrated peace and the romance of tribal stories to overcome the morose remembrance of the Wounded Knee Massacre. Could there have been a wiser resistance literature or simulation of survivance at the time? What did it mean to be the first generation to hear the stories of the past, bear the horrors of the moment, and write to the future? What were tribal identities at the turn of the last century?

"I made a promise to my grandfather never to lose touch with his Coast Salish traditions, never to abandon our cedar roots, never to forget any creature that shares this world, and never to allow or participate in a rape of the earth or the sea," wrote Duane Niatum in *I Tell You Now: Autobiographical Essays by Native American Writers*. Niatum, a poet and teacher, mentions that his surname was given to him by his great-aunt and recorded in court documents. "Because I feel this is a sacred trust, I have reason to suspect that if I live long enough, this name will turn out to be what ultimately changed my character and life."

Mary TallMountain, Koyukon Athabascan, the author of poems and stories who lives in San Francisco, wrote in the same collection of autobiographical essays, that "Alaska is my talisman, my strength, my spirit's home. Despite loss and dissolution, I count myself rich, fertile, and magical. I tell you now. You *can* go home again."

Native American Indian identities bear the tribal memories and solace of heard stories. Postindian identities are inscrutable recreations, the innermost brush with natural reason, and, at the same time, unbounded narcissism and a rush of new simulations of survivance.

The sources of tribal remembrance, tragic wisdom, creation, personal visions, and the communal nature of the heard are precarious, but the nuances of posted names are burdened more with colonial discoveries, duplicities, and simulations in the literature of dominance than with the menace of silence, the inaccuracies of memories and histories, or the uncertainties of stories out of season.

The distinctive salutations of a personal tribal nature, however, are more than the mere translation and possession of memories and names. Consider the untold influences and choices of names and metaphors of remembrance in specific cultural experiences, and the various sources of identities in public, private, intimate, and sacred circumstances; the choices become even more enigmatic with the vagaries, pleasures, and treasons of cultural contact, and the transvaluations of such wicked notions as savagism and civilization in the course of manifest manners and histories.

The literature of dominance, narratives of discoveries, translations, cultural studies, and prescribed names of time, place, and person are treacherous conditions in any discourse on tribal consciousness. Nature has no silence. The poses of silence are never natural, and other extremes, such as cultural revisionism, the ironic eminence of sacred consumer names, and assumed tribal nicknames, are dubious sources of consciousness; these distinctions, imitations, and other maneuvers are unsure stories heard over and over in common conversations.

The postindian warriors of simulations are not the insinuations of either humanism or "radical empiricism." Postindian simulations are the absence not the presence of the real, and neither simulations of survivance nor dominance resemble the pleasurable vagueness of consciousness.

William James wrote in *The Meaning of Truth* that one of the "main points of humanism" is that an "experience, perceptual or conceptual, must conform to reality in order to be true." Realities are preserved as the possible, but this would not embrace simulations because the real in humanism is not a contradiction of other realities.

"My present field of consciousness is a centre surrounded by a fringe that shades insensibly into a subconscious more," asserted James in *A Pluralistic Universe*. "I use three separate terms here to describe this fact; but I might as well use three hundred, for the fact is all shades and no boundaries."

Postindian simulations are the absence of shades, shadows, and consciousness; simulations are mere traces of common metaphors in the stories of survivance and the manners of domination.

Sacred names, those secure ceremonial names, were scarcely heard by missionaries or government agents and seldom translated as surnames; nicknames were assured in tribal stories, but the stories were lost in translation as surnames. Later, most surnames were chosen and dictated at federal and mission schools. Some tribal names endure in stories, and nicknames are identities learned and ascertained in language. Moreover, descriptive names seem to be more esteemed in translation, and certain choices of names are mere simulations with no memories or stories.

Luther Standing Bear was one of the first tribal students at the new government school at Carlisle, Pennsylvania. "One day when we came to school there was a lot of writing on one of the blackboards," he wrote in *My People the Sioux*. "We did not know what it meant, but our interpreter came into the room and said, 'Do you see all these marks on the blackboard? Well, each word is a white man. They are going to give each one of you one of these names by which you will hereafter be known.' None of the names were read or explained to us, so of course we did not know the sound or meaning of any of them. . . . I was one of the 'bright fellows' to learn my name quickly. How proud I was to answer when the teacher called the roll! I would put my blanket down and half raise myself in my seat, all ready to answer to my new name. I had selected the name 'Luther'—not 'Lutheran' as many people call me."

Captain Richard Pratt, who experimented with the education of tribal political prisoners at Fort Marion, Florida, became the first superintendent of the industrial school at Carlisle. He told the eleventh annual meeting of the Lake Mohonk Conference, three years after the massacre at Wounded Knee, that "the Indian has learned by long experience to believe somewhat that the only good white man is a dead white man, and he is just as right about it as any of us are in thinking the same of the Indian. It is only the Indian in them that ought to be killed; and it is the bad influences of the bad white man that ought to be killed too. How are these hindering, hurtful sentiments and conditions on both sides to be ended? Certainly, never by continuing the segregating policy, which gives the Indian no chance to see, know, and participate in our affairs and industries, and thus prove to himself and us that he has better stuff in him, and which prevents his learning how wrong is his conception of the truly civilized white man."

Luther and his generation were the last to hear the oral stories of their tribal families before the stories were translated, and they were the first to learn how to write about their remembrance and experiences.

The Indian became the other of manifest manners, the absence of the real tribes, the inventions in the literature of dominance. The postindian simulations of survivance, on the other hand, arose with a resistance literature. However, there are serious and notable distinctions in the comparison of tribal identities in the past century. Those tribal men and women who heard oral stories and then wrote their stories would not bear the same sources of consciousness as postindian warriors of simulations who are heard and written about by others.

Personal names and tribal nicknames are stories. "The idea that personal names might comprise a literary genre in some cultural contexts does not seem immediately obvious," wrote Peter Whiteley in his essay "Hopitutungwni: 'Hopi Names' as Literature." He points out that some Hopi names are "tiny imagist poems." The translation of nicknames would not reveal the obvious in tribal communities, the context and figuration of names in heard stories.

Snowarrow is but one recent name that has been chosen by a teacher to augment his tribal identities. Youngblood is another; some nicknames are ostentatious, and others are heard with no ascription. Some names are eschewed and others are renounced for countless reasons. Thomas Edward Kill, for instance, petitioned a court for permission to change his surname because he hoped to become a medical doctor and he did not think his tribal name in translation would inspire confidence.

Some names and associations are chance, to be sure, an ironic observance, or the break-even consciousness of apostates; for all that, tribal stories and natural reason are unanimous, memorable even in translation, and descriptive names are so celebrated in this generation that thousands of people pursue an obscure tribal connection, a passive wisp of ancestral descent in a name; others consume simulations and pretend, for various reasons, to be tribal in the name, blood, and remembrance of those who endured racialism and, with tragic wisdom, descried the literatures of dominance.

Native American Indian identities are created in stories, and names are essential to a distinctive personal nature, but memories, visions, and the shadows of heard stories are the paramount verities of a tribal presence. The shadows are active and intransitive, the visual memories that are heard as tribal stories; these memories are trusted to sacred names and tribal nicknames.

Tribal consciousness would be a minimal existence without active choices, the choices that are heard in stories and mediated in names; otherwise, tribal identities might be read as mere simulations of remembrance. Manifest manners are dubious entitlements to the names and stories in other cultures; the simulations that antecede traces in literature and shadows of the real are the simulations that unteach the mediations of tribal names and stories.

Luther Standing Bear, for instance, chose his names, and the stories of the bear are heard even in the translation of his surname. He wrote in *My Indian Boyhood* that "the Indian very seldom bothers a bear and the bear, being a very self-respecting and peaceful animal, seldom bothers a human being." The bear is the shadow in the memories and the trace in his names. The bear is "so much like a human that he is interesting to watch." The bear is "wise and clever and he probably knows it."

Not only is the bear "a powerful animal in body, but powerful in will also." The bear "will not run, but will die fighting. Because my father shared this spirit with the bear, he earned his name," wrote Standing Bear. "While in battle he was badly wounded, yet with blood streaming from his body, he did not give up and for this bravery earned a name of which he was ever after proud."

Standing Bear mentioned the caution of hunters because of the "bear dreamers" of the tribe. "They are the medicine men who, during their fast, have had a vision in which the bear had come to them and revealed a useful herb or article with which to cure the sick." N. Scott Momaday, the novelist, wrote in *The Way to Rainy Mountain* that his tribal grandmother "lived out her long life in the shadow of Rainy Mountain, the immense landscape of the continental interior lay like memory in her blood. . . . I wanted to see in reality what she had seen more perfectly in the mind's eye." Aho, his grandmother, heard the oral stories of a migration that lasted five centuries; she could hear and see a landscape in imagination, and these stories became the shadows of tribal remembrance.

Momaday honors the memories of his grandmother and touches the shadows of his own imagination, shadows that trace his identities and tribal stories in three scriptural themes in *The Way to Rainy Mountain*.

Tribal nicknames are the shadows heard in stories; the pleasures of nicknames, even in translation, are an unmistakable celebration of personal identities. Nicknames are personal stories that would, to be sure, trace the individual to tribal communities rather than cause separations by pronouns of singular recognition.

Brian Swann and Arnold Krupat, the editors of *I Tell You Now*, a collection of autobiographical essays by tribal writers, pointed out that "the notion of telling the whole of any one individual's life or taking merely personal experience as of particular significance was, in the most literal way, foreign to them, if not also repugnant." Nothing, however, is foreign or repugnant in personal names and the stories of nicknames. The risks, natural reasons, and praise of visions are sources of personal power in tribal consciousness; personal stories are coherent and name individual identities within communities, and are not an obvious opposition to communal values.

The shadows of personal visions, for instance, were heard and seen alone, but not in cultural isolation or separation from tribal communities. Those who chose to hear visions, an extreme mediation, were aware that their creative encounters with nature were precarious and would be sanctioned by the tribe; personal visions could be of service to tribal families. Some personal visions and stories have the power to heal and liberate the spirit, and there are similar encounters with tribal shadows in the stories by contemporary tribal authors.

Nicknames, shadows, and shamanic visions are tribal stories that are heard and remembered as survivance. These personal identities and stories are not the same as those translated in the literature of dominance.

"My spirit was quiet there," Momaday wrote in *The Names*, a meticulous memoir of his childhood at Jemez, New Mexico. "The silence was old, immediate, and pervasive, and there was great good in it. The wind of the canyons drew it out; the voices of the village carried and were lost in it. Much was made of the silence; much of the summer and winter was made of it."

"I tell parts of my stories here because I have often searched out other lives similar to my own," wrote Linda Hogan in *I Tell You Now*, edited by Brian Swann and Arnold Krupat. "Telling our lives is important, for those who come after us, for those who will see our experience as part of their own historical struggle."

"I was raised by an English-German mother. My father, one-quarter Cherokee, was there also, but it was my mother who presented her white part of my heritage as whole," wrote Diane Glancy in *I Tell You Now*. "I knew I was different, then as much as now. But I didn't know until later that it was because I am part heir to the Indian culture, and even that small part has leavened the whole lump."

"Facts: May 7, 1948. Oakland. Catholic Hospital. Midwife nun, no doctor. Citation won the Kentucky Derby. Israel was born. The United Nations met for the first time," wrote Wendy Rose in *I Tell You Now*. "I have heard Indians joke about those who act as if they had no relatives. I wince, because I have no relatives. They live, but they threw me away. . . . I am without relations. I have always swung back and forth between alienation and relatedness."

The postindian first person pronoun is a salutation to at least nine simulations of tribal identities in the literature of dominance. The simulations are the practices, conditions, characteristics, and the manifold nature of tribal experiences. The simulations would include tribal documentation, peer recognition, sacred names and nicknames, cultural anxieties, crossblood assurance, nationalism, pantribalism, new tribalism, and reservation residence.

*   The inheritance of tribal traits and the traditional use of an oral tribal language, recognition of peers, and documents of family connections to a reservation or tribal community are simulations of identities.

*   Tribal nicknames are heard in oral stories; the names are given by others and are associated with communities, not the separate and autistic induction of the individual. The translation of nicknames as surnames is the closure of tribal stories and the remembrance of communities in the association of names and pronouns; translated names are misconstrued identities in the literature of dominance.

*   The historicism of tribal cultures and the indispensable linear representations of time, place, and person, in the absence of the real are simulations of manifest manners.

*   The manifold anxieties and desires that arise from the tension announced in the binary of savagism and civilization are other simulations in the literature of dominance.

*   The notions of crossbloodism, determinism, and racialism, maintain the sentiments of weakness, that crossbloods are a descent from pure racial simulations.

*   The manifest manners of nationalism as sources of tribal identities are both means of association and resistance; some tribes are simulated as national cultural emblems, and certain individuals are honored by the nation and the tribe as *real* representations.

*   Pantribalism, an institutional and personal simulation, presents a source of identities for tribal governments and professionals, such as tribal teachers and medical doctors, and a common source of

individual recognition and association for those who have no other sources of tribal identities; pantribal associations are common at universities and tribal community centers in cities.

* Tribalism is an essential source of identities; the notion that tribal identities are inherited as a universal connection in the blood determines political and cultural unities in the literature of dominance.

* The reservation simulations are the notion that reservation experiences determine obvious tribal identities. Thousands of tribal people have moved from reservations to cities in the past century to avoid poverty, sexual abuse, and the absence of services, education, and employment.

Nationalism is the most monotonous simulation of dominance in first person pronouns of tribal consciousness. The stories of tribal names chase new metaphors as the simulations of survivance. Homi Bhabha argued in "DissemiNation: time, narrative, and the margins of the modern nation," an essay on the "strategies of cultural identification" in *Narration and Nation*, that the "nation fills the void left in the uprooting of communities and kin, and turns that loss into the language of metaphor."

The concerted creations of tribal cultures are in continuous translations as stories, and the situation of hermeneutics remains the same in simulations; the silence of heard stories in translations, and the absence of the heard, antecedes a presence in the shadows of names. Has the absence of the heard in tribal stories turned to the literatures of dominance? What are the real names, nouns, and pronouns heard in the fields of tribal consciousness? How can a pronoun be a source of tribal identities in translation? How can a pronoun be essential, an inscription of absence that represents the presence of sound and a person in translation?

Hertha Dawn Wong declared an obscure connection to tribal identities in the preface to *Sending My Heart Back Across the*

Years, a study of "nonwritten forms of personal narratives." She wrote that "according to the Oklahoma Historical Society, my great-grandfather may have been Creek or Chickasaw or Choctaw or perhaps Cherokee." That whimsical sense of chance, "may have been" one of four or more distinct tribes, is not an answerable choice or source of credible identities. "I had little idea," when she began writing her book, "that I was part Native American, one of the unidentified mixed-bloods whose forebears wandered away from their fractured communities, leaving little cultural trace in their adopted world." The racialism of these romantic notions would bear minimal honor in tribal memories.

Elizabeth Cook-Lynn, editor of *Wicazo Sa Review*, argued that the "wannabee sentiment" that clutters *Sending My Heart Back Across the Years* "is a reflection of a growing phenomenon" at universities in "the name of Native American Studies." The "unnecessary claim of this scholar to be 'part Native American' is so absurd as to cast ridicule on the work itself." She pointed out that curriculum development at universities "has been reduced to offerings which might be called 'What If I'm a Little Bit Indian?' " The pretensions of some scholars, however, are not even a little bit tribal.

Jack Anderson, in a column released by the Universal Press Syndicate in 1984, reported of Jamake Highwater that "one of the country's most celebrated Indians has fabricated much of the background that made him famous." Highwater, the columnist revealed, "lied about many details of his life. Asked why someone of such genuine and extraordinary talent felt he had to concoct a spurious background, Highwater said he felt that doors would not have opened for him if he had relied on his talent alone." Anderson pointed out that "Vine Deloria Jr. and Hank Adams say flatly that Highwater is not an Indian."

Highwater, author of *The Primal Mind* and other books about tribal cultures, may have opened doors with his spurious identities, but he also stole public attention, and his bent for recognition may have closed some doors on honest tribal people who have the moral courage to raise doubts about identities. "The greatest mystery of my life is my own identity," Highwater wrote in *Shadow Show: An Autobiographical Insinuation*, published two years after the column by Jack Anderson. "To escape things that are painful we must reinvent ourselves. Either we reinvent ourselves or we choose not to be anyone at all. We must not feel guilty if we are among those who have managed to survive."

Highwater insinuated six years earlier that he was of tribal descent. "As Indians, we are extensions of a people. I am not a person, I am a people, a Blackfeet. I am one aspect of a rainbow, part of a whole spectrum. I don't make any sense by myself," he wrote in *This Song Remembers*, edited by Jane Katz. "I care what happens to Indian people. I feel that we are a spiritual body. We are dreamers; we believe in dreams." Undeniably, he was a dreamer about his tribal descent, but the concoction of tribal identities is dishonorable; the course of manifest manners and the literature of dominance.

Anthony Kerby argued in *Narrative and the Self* that the loss of the "ability to narrate one's past is tantamount to a form of amnesia, with a resultant diminishing of one's sense of self. Why should this be so? The answer, broadly stated, is that our history constitutes a drama in which we are a leading character, and the meaning of this role is to be found only through the recollective and imaginative configuring of that history in autobiographical acts. In other words, in narrating the past we understand ourselves to be the implied subject generated by the narrative."

In other words, tribal identities are heard in names and stories; otherwise the simulations that antecede tribal stories and tragic wisdom would be tantamount to amnesia and the discoveries of tribal cultures in the literatures of dominance.

SHADOW SURVIVANCE

The postindian turns in literature, the later indication of new narratives, are an invitation to the closure of dominance in the ruins of representation. The invitation uncovers traces of tribal survivance, trickster hermeneutics, and the remanence of intransitive shadows.

The traces are shadows, shadows, shadows, the natural reach of shadows, memories, and visions in heard stories. The postindian simulations and shadows counter the dominance of histories and the dickered testimonies of representations; at the same time, trickster stories, transformations, and the shimmers of tribal consciousness are heard in the literature of survivance.

Linda Hutcheon wrote in *The Politics of Postmodernism* that the "representation of history becomes the history of representation." She pointed out that the "issue of representation in both fiction and history has usually been dealt with in epistemological terms, in terms of how we know the past."

The representations of the past are more than mere human mimesis in the prenarrative dimensions of tribal lives, and more than the aesthetic remains of reason in the literature of dominance. The posers, of course, must concentrate on the sources of incoherence that trace causation in transitive histories. Simulations of the tribal real and the colonial arrogance that precedes a tribal referent are the most common representations in histories. The simulations of manifest manners are new burdens in the absence of the real and the imposture of presence.

"Our identity is that of a particular historical being, and this identity can persist only through the continued integration of ongoing experience," wrote Anthony Kerby in *Narrative and the Self*. We are the experiences and the narrators, and "because we bring our history along with us, as a more or less clearly configured horizon, new experiences will tend to flow into this story of our lives, augmenting it and adapting themselves to it."

Postindian consciousness is a rush of shadows in the distance, and the trace of natural reason to a bench of stones; the human silence of shadows, and animate shadows over presence. The shadow is that sense of intransitive motion to the referent; the silence in memories. Shadows are neither the absence of entities nor the burden of conceptual references. The shadows are the prenarrative silence that inherits the words; shadows are the motions that mean the silence, but not the presence or absence of entities. The sounds of words, not the entities of shadows and natural reason, are limited in human consciousness and the distance of discourse. Shadows are honored in memories and the silence of tribal stones.

I hear the push of the wind in late summer, in the winter birch, and see the shadows hie over the shore in silence; and my shadows move with the light, the sources of remembrance. We are shadows, silence, stones, stories, never that simulation of light in the distance. Trickster stones and postindian stories are my shadows, the natural traces of liberation and survivance in the ruins of representation.

"Every man casts a shadow; not his body only, but his imperfectly mingled spirit," wrote Henry David Thoreau in *A Week on the Concord and Merrimack Rivers*. "This is his grief. Let him turn which way he will, it falls opposite to the sun; short at noon, long at eve."

Thoreau observed that "most objects will cast a shadow wider than themselves." Shadows and remembrance are the diffusion of light in silence, and at an eternal distance from the sun, as if our stories were shadows that rushed to that elusive union of shadows and light.

Thoreau craved the summer shadows on the pond; he heard the turn of the seasons as he would stones, and the light landed with his hands, the generous shadows of the morning. "I did not read books the first summer; I hoed beans," he wrote later in *Walden.* "Nay, I often did better than this. There were times when I could not afford to sacrifice the bloom of the present moment to any work, whether of the head or hands. I love a broad margin to my life."

The shadows of remembrance and survivance are borrowed metaphors then, an "imperfectly mingled spirit." Shadows and their words create the seasons; the intransitive shadows that touch a distance, the absence, and prenarrative silence.

The haiku poem, for instance, ascribes the seasons with shadow words: the light that turns a leaf, a bird, a hand. Shadow words are intuitive, a concise mediation of sound, motion, memories, and the sensation of the seasons. "Haiku is the result of the wish, the effort, not to speak, not to write poetry, not to obscure further the truth and suchness of a thing with words, with thoughts and feelings," wrote R. H. Blyth in *Haiku.*

V. S. Naipaul envisioned the separation of shadow words and remembrance in the essence of jasmine. He stuck a sprig in the buttonhole of his shirt and smelled the flower as he walked back to the hotel. "Jasmine, jasmine," he wrote. "But the word and the flower had been separate in my mind for too long. They did not come together."

Naipaul, in his essay "Jasmine," remembered his youth in Trinidad, observed Timothy Weiss in *On the Margins,* and "he was familiar with the scent of the flower without knowing its name, which belonged to other contexts: *jasmine* was 'a word in a book, a word to play with, something removed from the dull vegetation.' While the plant belonged to the West Indian landscape, its name was part of his

British education and the romance of his literary ambitions." Naipaul "expresses his sense of divided reality deriving from a linguistic, cultural, and economic inheritance as a colonial." The colonial inheritance, however, is the recourse of the word, not the scent of jasmine; the word is a shadow not the closure of remembrance.

There are at least four postmodern conditions in the critical responses to Native American Indian and postindian literatures: the first is heard in aural performances; the second is unbodied in translations; the third is the trickster hermeneutics of liberation, the uncertain humor and shimmer of survivance that denies the obscure maneuvers of manifest manners, tragic transvaluations, and the incoherence of cultural representations; the fourth is narrative chance, the counter causes in language games, consumer simulations, and the histories of publications since the removal of tribal communities to federal exclaves or reservations.

These four conditions turn a diverse discourse on tribal literatures: the uncertain testimonies, the remanence of shadows, and tribal transvaluations; the enigmatic nature of memories, imagination, and autobiographies; the translation of nicknames, picture fictions, or memorial expressionism, and shamanic visions; the tragic flaws and denials of tribal wisdom in the literature of dominance, and the morass of social science surveillance and theories; the enervation of modernism; the rise of simulations and manifest manners, that vernacular of racialism and continuous elaborations on the rights, responsibilities, and the dubious duties of dominance.

These postmodern conditions are both oppositional and noetic mediations on narrative chance; these conditions are an invitation to the postindian simulations of tribal survivance. The traces of natural reason and the shadows of coherence have endured over science in the humor of cotribal stories.

"Science has always been in conflict with narratives," wrote Jean-François Lyotard in *The Postmodern Condition*. "I define postmod-

ern as incredulity toward metanarratives." Science, translation, and
the discoveries of otherness in tribal cultures are the histories of
racialism and the metanarratives of dominance. The foundational
theories of the social sciences have denied natural reason, tribal
memories, and the coherence of heard stories. Lyotard argued that
"knowledge has become the principal force of production over the
last few decades." The literature of dominance maintains the scientific
models and tragic simulations of a consumer culture.

We must "achieve a knowledge of language from inside of language, as linguistic beings, as opposed to the scientific notion of a
knowledge of nature from outside of nature, as detached individuals," wrote Will Wright in *Wild Knowledge*. He argued that "from
the inside, language formally organizes our ability to know our world,
and this ability depends upon our understanding ourselves as capable
of effective, sustainable interactions with our world. Thus from the
inside language imposes formal conceptual conditions on our understanding of ourselves and our world."

Linda Hutcheon pointed out that accession to the past in fiction
and histories is through the traces of "documents, the testimony of
witnesses, and other archival materials. In other words, we only have
representations of the past from which to construct our narratives
or explanations. In a very real sense, postmodernism reveals a desire
to understand present culture as the product of previous representations." This narrow accession would burden the narratives of chance
and the shadows of tribal survivance.

Richard Rorty pointed out in *Contingency, irony, and solidarity*,
that the words of our lives are a "final vocabulary" with "no non-
circular argumentative recourse" because, in this sense, language becomes an essential border. "All human beings carry about a set of
words which they employ to justify their actions, their beliefs, and
their lives. These are the words in which we formulate praise of our
friends and contempt for our enemies. . . . the words in which we tell,

sometimes prospectively and sometimes retrospectively, the story of our lives. I shall call these words a person's 'final vocabulary.' "

Rorty observed that the common sense of final vocabularies is the opposite of the doubt and renunciation of ironies. The ironist "thinks nothing has an intrinsic nature, a real essence." Science, justice, and other terms, are final vocabularies in the language games of our time. "The ironist spends her time worrying about the possibility that she has been initiated into the wrong tribe, taught to play the wrong language game. She worries that the process of socialization which turned her into a human being by giving her a language may have given her the wrong language, and so turned her into the wrong kind of human being."

Shadow words are the hermeneutics of survivance. The postindian is an ironist who worries about names, manners, and stories. The shadows in trickster stories would overturn the terminal vernacular of manifest manners, and the final vocabularies of dominance.

The ironies and humor in the postmodern are heard in tribal narratives; the natural reason of tribal creation has never been without a postmodern turn or counterpoise, a common mode that enlivened the performance and memories of those who heard the best of their own experiences in stories. The shadows of the heard and that touch of coherence in natural reason persist in the postindian literature of resistance and in the stories that are told at the end of federal exclaves and reservations.

Native American Indian literatures could be read as the eternal shadows of the heard rather than as mere evidence, and as the serious wisps of natural reason in postindian narratives. These narrative wisps are the "stories that one tells, that one hears, that one acts out," wrote Lyotard, "the people does not exist as a subject but as a mass of millions of insignificant and serious little stories that sometimes let themselves be collected together to constitute big stories and sometimes disperse into digressive elements."

Social science narratives, those unsure reins of final vocabularies and incoherent paracolonialism, overscore the tribal heard as cultural representations. David Carroll argued in *The Subject in Question* that any "narrative that predetermines all responses or prohibits any counter-narratives puts an end to narrative itself, by making itself its own end and the end of all other narratives."

Johannes Fabian, the anthropologist, conceded in the introduction to *Language and Colonial Power* that he lost his faith in the assumption that language is a representation of a real world. That assumption has been one of the foundations of the social sciences and colonial dominance. Concessions and antitheses are an invitation to a discourse on racialism, but at the same time the "assumptions" of foundational representations have become the simulations of the real and serve a consumer paradise in the literature of dominance.

The wild unities of heard stories and the pleasures of performance are unbodied in translations. The shadows and tribal experiences that are *heard* in stories, and variations on natural reason, are transformed in publications that are *seen* as cultural representations. The conditions of postindian identities must sue for more than revisions in the new historicism.

Native American Indian literatures have endured the manifest manners of translation for more than three centuries. The sudden closures of the oral in favor of the scriptural are unheard, and the eternal sorrow of lost sounds haunts the remains of tribal stories in translation. Brian Swann, in an edited collection of essays on translation, explained that given "the history of this hemisphere, to settle for the dignity of mystery is far preferable to any claim of definitiveness."

Modernism, a persuasive disguise of aesthetic individualism, is the tragic flaw of historicism. The postmodern condition, then, is a counterpoise in "wild knowledge" and language games, an invitation to a "reflexive nature" that would undermine the trust of presence in translation, representation, and simulations. Natural reason and a reflexive nature are virtues of the literature of survivance.

"Scientific knowledge has lost its objective privilege and its epistemology has collapsed into incoherence, and yet our social theories continue to grant it analytic privilege," wrote Will Wright in *Wild Knowledge.* "I am arguing that the scientific ideas of knowledge and nature are incoherent." Moreover, "nature must be understood reflexively, through a reference to language, not objectively," and "rationality must be criticized in the name of reflexive nature, not accepted in the name of objective nature."

What has been published and seen is not what is heard or remembered in oral stories. Postindian narratives are poses, and the poses are neither representations nor the terminal sources of aesthetic modernism. The printed word has no natural evolution in tribal literatures. The heard words are traced in silence, the shadows of tribal memories, and the printed words reach over presence and absence to the shadows of trees, water, air, and hear stone, hide, and paper, as words have been heard forever in tribal stories.

The representations of the heard are simulations, no more than nuances in the best translations. Representation, and the obscure maneuvers of translation, "produces strategies of containment." These strategies are "deployed across a wide range of discourses, allowing us to name translation as a significant technology of colonial domination," argued Tejaswini Niranjana in *Siting Translation.* "Paradoxically, translation also provides a place in 'history' for the colonized." The histories are texts in the literature of dominance, and the shadows of the heard emerge from the *différance* and traces of the texts.

Jacques Derrida turns his *différance* to overread the dash, variance, and indeterminate traces that misconstrue the past representations of presence and absence in written literature. The causal compromises of objectivization in transitive actions are the terminal poses of presence and the past. Shadows and oral stories arise in tribal silence and are heard in that aural distance to the chance concept, that reach of lonesome silence between the signifier, the signified, and their signs; the traces and *différance* of meaning are dashed and deferred to the silence of other texts in the literature of dominance. Shadows are that silence and sense of motion in memories; shadows are not the burdens of conceptual references. Shadows and *différance* in other texts threaten the representations of presence and the run on simulations. Not even the tease of trace and *différance* is answerable to the tone and dissemblance of scriptural, hermeneutical, and representational translations of the heard stories. The shadows are heard in names and stories but not as mere representations. The shadows of tribal memories are the active silence, trace, and *différance* in the literature of survivance.

The "charge of 'linguistic idealism' has probably been the accusation most frequently leveled against deconstruction over the years," wrote Richard Wolin in *The Terms of Cultural Criticism*. "Derrida's approach to criticism, argues Foucault, remains exclusively *textual*. As an interpreter and critic, he leads us into the text from which, in turn, *we never emerge*."

"Not only is there no kingdom of *différance*, but *différance* instigates the subversion of every kingdom. Which makes it obviously threatening and infallibly dreaded by everything within us that desires a kingdom," Derrida wrote in "*Différance*." Jacques Derrida is an indirect reflexive trace to his own *différance* and absence in deconstruction. Shadows are over the sounds, words, and traces. The shadows and traces are silence, but shadows and silence are not the trace. Shadows are motion not presence, shadows touch no presence or absence over sound and sentences.

"Presence is reduced to signs of itself—to traces," wrote Raymond Tallis in *Not Saussure*. "We never touch presence unmediated by signs—immediate presence, presence itself. Mediation is primary; immediacy but an impossible, elusive dream."

Allen Thiher, in *Words in Reflection*, argued that signs are not representations. "Signs derive their identity and meaning from their position in the space of the linguistic system: this position can be defined only by their opposition to and difference from other signs." Michel Foucault observed in *The Order of Things* that "the relation of the sign to the signified now resides in a space in which there is no longer any intermediary figure to connect them: what connects them is a bond established, inside knowledge, between the *idea of one thing* and the *idea of another*." Signs are "set free" and then confined in representation, "in the interstices of ideas, in that narrow space in which they interact with themselves in a perpetual state of decomposition and recomposition."

The classical notion that thoughts were representations of content, or the coherent meaning of words, is not the same as the nature of shadows in tribal names and stories. Shadows tease and loosen the bonds of representation in stories. The meaning of words are determined by the nature of language games.

"As signs, words now belong to a separate ontological realm," wrote Gary Gutting in *Michel Foucault's archaeology of scientific reason*. "Language is no longer intertwined with the world, a reality of the same nature as the things it signifies. It ceases to resemble and instead represents. . . . The representations of language express a content that they themselves do not possess. An important epistemological consequence is that erudition ceases to be a form of knowledge. This is because words can no longer be regarded as natural signs forming a part of the world, including in it as marks of the truth."

The natural world is a venture of sound and shadows, and the outcome of the oral tradition is not the silence of discoveries, dominance, and written narratives. The natural development of the oral tradition is not a written language. The notion, in the literature of dominance, that the oral advances to the written, is a colonial reduction of natural sound, heard stories, and the tease of shadows in tribal remembrance.

The trace is a nickname that leaves a presence in literature. The shadows are the silence in heard stories, the silence that bears a referent of tribal memories and experience. The shadow words are active memories, and the memories of heard stories. The shadows are intransitive, an animate action in the silence of stories. The word *agawaatese* is heard in the oral stories of the *anishinaabe*, the tribal people of the northern woodland lakes. The word hears silence and shadows, and could mean a shadow, or casts a shadow. The sense of *agawaatese* is that the shadows are animate entities. The shadow is the unsaid presence in names, the memories in silence, and the imagination of tribal experiences.

N. Scott Momaday, for instance, wrote in his memoir, *The Names*, about the shadow and sense of presence in a name. "Mammadaty was my grandfather, whom I never knew. Yet he came to be imagined posthumously in the going on of the blood, having invested the shadow of his presence in an object or a word, in his name above all. He enters into my dreams; he persists in his name."

Luther Standing Bear wrote in *My Indian Boyhood* that the bear is "so much like a human that he is interesting to watch. He has a large amount of human vanity and likes to look at himself. Before we had looking-glasses, we would look at ourselves in a clear pool of water. This the bear does, too, and I suppose he thinks, 'Well, I'm not such a bad-looking fellow,' for he walks away after an inspection of himself as if quite satisfied, and as for myself I do not see why he should not be. He is wise and clever and probably knows it."

The bear is a shadow in tribal memories and heard stories. The sound, silence, and shadows of the bear are animate and intransitive. The shadows, silence, and unsaid presence of bears end in the course of signification; shadows and silence have no representations, no presence, no absence, no antishadows.

The bear is a shadow in the silence of tribal stories; memories and that sense of presence are unsaid in the name. Luther Standing Bear hears the shadow of the bear in his memories; the bear is a shadow and has no presence in heard stories or in the silence of the written name. The bear he hears, reads, and writes is a shadow of the bear, not the real bear, not a mere concept of the bear, but the shadow memories of the bear. The shadow, not the bear, is the referent, the sense of presence in the name, and the trace to other stories.

The bear "will stand and fight to the last. Though wounded, he will not run, but will die fighting. Because my father shared this spirit with the bear, he earned his name," wrote Standing Bear. The shadows in the name are the memories in the shadow of the bear and the silence in translation. The name is heard and read, and there are traces and *différance* that defer the meaning, but without the stories of the bear and the name the shadow has no memories in the silence of translation.

"Although my grandmother lived out her long life in the shadow of Rainy Mountain, the immense landscape of the continental interior lay like memory in her blood. She could tell of the Crows, whom she had never seen, and of the Black Hills, where she had never been," N. Scott Momaday wrote in *The Way to Rainy Mountain*. "I wanted to see in reality what she had seen more perfectly in the mind's eye, and traveled fifteen hundred miles to begin my pilgrimage." Aho, his tribal grandmother, heard stories of the long migration of the tribe, and these stories became her memories in imagination, so that she could hear the shadows of a landscape that she had never seen. The shadows are the creations of the tribe, and shadows are memories that are heard in stories. Shadows, memories, and imagination endure in the silence of translation.

"There is a perfect freedom in the mountains, but it belongs to the eagle and the elk, the badger and the bear. The Kiowas reckoned their stature by the distance they could see, and they were bent and blinded in the wilderness," wrote Momaday.

Native American Indian literatures have been overburdened with critical interpretations based on structuralism and other social science theories that value incoherent foundational representations of tribal experiences. Brian Swann and Arnold Krupat pointed out in *Recovering the Word* that structuralism, a "concern for principles of organization and function," dominated their edited collection of critical essays on Native American literatures. The "Indian as an individual is not much examined in these essays."

Claude Lévi-Strauss and Alan Dundas have been cited more than Mikhail Bakhtin, Jean-François Lyotard, or Jacques Derrida in the historical and critical studies of tribal literature; the theoretical persuasions have been more structural and representational than postmodern in the past few decades of translation and interpretation. Foundational theories have overburdened tribal imagination, memories, and the coherence of natural reason with simulations and the cruelties of paracolonial historicism. Anthropologists, in particular, were not the best listeners or interpreters of tribal imagination, liberation, or literatures.

The elusive and clever trickster characters in tribal imagination are seldom heard or understood in translation. Missionaries and anthropologists were the first to misconstrue silence, transformation, and figuration in tribal stories; they were not trained to hear stories as creative literature and translated many stories as mere cultural representations. Victor Barnouw, for example, wrote in *Wisconsin Chippewa Myths & Tales* that from trickster stories "we can learn something about the belief systems of the people." He misconstrued the trickster as "a real person whom they respected although they also laughed at his antics."

Barnouw reduced the oral trickster stories that he heard to unreasonable social science evidence and cultural representations; moreover, an analysis of the storyteller concluded that "there was evidence of emotional dependency and also some confusion about sex." This outrageous interpretation was based on a Rorschach record.

Karl Kroeber pointed out in *Traditional American Indian Literatures* that anthropologists and "folklorists, whose disciplines are not directed toward appreciation of superior artistry, usually play down, or ignore, the individual distinction of creative accomplishment in ethnographic material."

Moreover, anthropologists have used the inventions of ethnic cultures and the representations of the tribes as tropes to academic power in institutions. "The critical issue, so far as concerns the anthropologist as author, works and lives, text-building, and so on, is the highly distinctive representation of 'being there' that *Tristes Tropiques* develops, and the equally distinctive representation, invertive actually, of the relationship between referring text and referred-to world that follows from it," wrote Clifford Geertz in *Words and Lives.* "To put it brutally, but not inaccurately, Lévi-Strauss argues that the sort of immediate, in-person 'being there' one associates with the bulk of recent American and British anthropology is essentially impossible: it is either outright fraud or fatuous self-deception. The notion of a continuity between experience and reality, he says early on in *Tristes Tropiques*, is false: 'there is no continuity in the passage between the two.'"

Native American Indian imagination and the pleasures of language games are disheartened in the manifest manners of documentation and the imposition of cultural representation; tribal testimonies are unheard, and tricksters, the wild ironies of survivance, transformation, natural reason, and liberation in stories, are marooned as obscure moral simulations in translations.

Andrew Wiget, for instance, declared that the behavior of the trickster is "always scandalous. His actions were openly acknowledged as madness by the elders who performed the stories with obvious relish on many winter evenings. Yet these same respected voices would solemnly assert the sacredness of these very tales, which always involved the most cavalier treatment of conventionally unassailable material like sexuality or religion." Wiget, a literary scholar, bears the worst of colonial historicism in his interpretations of trickster figuration in tribal literature. "To many Westerners reading these stories for the first time, it seemed at best a puzzling inconsistency and at worst a barbaric mystery that in many tribal mythologies this idiot and miscreant was in some unaccountable way also the culture hero."

Wiget, in turn, could be read as a modern moral censor, an overman of occidental binaries and the tropes to academic power. The tone of his critical attention in *Native American Literature*, and the use of the words *scandalous* and *barbaric*, would prescribe a righteous paracolonial presence in tribal stories. The trickster is a language game, a counter causal liberation of the mind, not salvation or the measure of representation and invented cultural values.

Wiget is a sincere exponent, to be sure, but he has undermined the natural reason and creative power of tribal literatures with his use of structuralism and other social science theories; he has that, and much more, in common with other scholars who have translated and interpreted tribal literatures.

Wiget comes closer to modernism and the social sciences than to other critical theories in his interpretations of tribal literature; he separates tribal stories with morphologies and genre representations. In *Native American Literature* he covers the tribal world from oral narratives to the novel in six short chapters. Alas, he announced that "trying to find some clear and universal criteria for distinguishing different types of narrative has been the ever-elusive goal of folklorists and anthropologists." He asserted that oral cultures were not static, but at the same time he explained that "there has been no single effort to order and assess that literature."

The Native American Indian "implicitly acknowledged he could continue living only in the white man's representation of him," wrote the historian Larzer Ziff in *Writing in the New Nation*. "The process of literary annihilation would be checked only when Indian writers began representing their own culture." However, even then most readers and critics influenced by structuralism, modernism, and the dualism of subject, object, or otherness have more confidence in the paracolonial discoveries and representations of tribal literatures. Familiar simulations have more in common with the philosophies of grammar and translations than with shadows and the silence of heard stories in the unbearable simulations of tribal consciousness.

Translation, in another sense, is a monothematic representation of silence and distance. Published stories move in silence over time, but that silence is never secure. Time is a measure of boredom and dominance, and those who translate oral stories are marooned with time in the ruins of representation. The shadows of heard stories are not bound by the measures of time and space. The presence of sign language was lost in speech and written languages. Sign language and postindian literatures are the simulations of survivance.

"When sign language gave way to interpreted speech, even as the recorded facts and unmediated impressions of the travelers gave way to the written history of the expedition, so cultural equality gave way to dominance and the process of literary annihilation," wrote Larzer Ziff. "Since signs are not grounded in words, those who use them recognize the limits of what they can express and thus of the understanding they can achieve. While this restricts their communication to elementary things, it also promotes an equality between them."

Sacajawea, and others, "acquired their second languages at the cost of their freedom," argued Ziff. "Captivity was the precondition for intertribal linguistic exchange within oral cultures. This cause and effect relationship, however, was reversed within the written culture of Americans."

The "power of language is one of N. Scott Momaday's most enduring themes," Wiget wrote about *House Made of Dawn*. "Momaday is breaking new ground with his intensely personal, poetic narratives, which essay the principal dilemma of an urbanized, thoroughly acculturated Indian: how to retain continuity with one's cultural heritage though displaced from the community that sustains it. The very structures of these works express the dynamic by which the psyche internalizes the mythic, historical, and cultural components of identity."

Winter in the Blood by James Welch is "a hopeful book," wrote Wiget. "In the mock-epic struggle to rescue the mired cow, there are signs of a recovery of commitment to life to replace the internalized distance." The consumer notion of a "hopeful book" is a denial of tragic wisdom and seems to be a social science paradise of the antiselves in manifest manners.

"She was lying on her side, up to her chest in mud," said the unnamed narrator in *Winter in the Blood*. The cow "had earned this fate by being stupid, and now no one could help her. . . . As she stared at me, I saw beyond the immediate panic that hatred, that crazy hatred that made me aware of a quick hatred in my own heart. Her horns seemed tipped with blood, the dark blood of catastrophe." She turned her head in the mud, one eye to the clouds. That laconic sense of chance and death bears tribal ironies and tragic wisdom; the postindian characters and scenes are more than victims and mock separations.

"Once one abandons the idea that all Indian novelists must be angry, it is not surprising to find that *Winter in the Blood* has a strong comic undercurrent," wrote Alan Velie in *Four American Indian Literary Masters*. "The comic novel is becoming the dominant genre in fiction today." Velie was the first scholar to observe the comic and ironic themes in Native American Indian literature. His interpretations were literary, a wise departure from the surveillance of the social sciences. The tribes were tragic, never comic, or ironic, in the literature of dominance.

Louis Owens pointed out in *Other Destinies* that "only nine novels by American Indian authors had been published" before *House Made of Dawn* in 1968. "The first was John Rollin Ridge's *Joaquin Murieta* in 1854, followed by Simon Pokagon's *Queen of the Woods* in 1899, Mourning Dove's *Cogewea, the Half-Blood* in 1927, three novels by the Cherokee writer John Milton Oskison in the 1920s and 1930s, John Joseph Mathews's *Sundown* in 1934, and D'Arcy McNickle's *The Surrounded* in 1936 and *Runner in the Sun* in 1954. However, as if Momaday had triggered a long-dormant need among Indian writers, the 1970s saw the publication of a stream of novels by Indian authors. . . . In more than a century of American Indian novels, an evolution has taken place in the way Indian writers approach their subjects and the way these novels fit into the mainstream of American literature."

Charles Larson studied three generations of fiction writers in *American Indian Fiction*. He started with a review of *Queen of the Woods* by Simon Pokagon, one of the first Native American Indian novels published at the turn of the last century, and ended with *Ceremony* by Leslie Marmon Silko. His book was the first serious critical interpretation of published fiction by more than sixty authors identified as Native American Indians. Larson inherited the manifest manners of dominance; however, racialism determined the measures of tribal identities. The obscure notions of blood quantums, that arithmetic reduction of neat bloodlines, were dubious and uncertain measures of identities; so, in the end, he decided that the known "acceptance by one's peers" was a "more meaningful test of Indianness."

Larson invented four categories of states, traits, and advocates, to describe the novelists and their publications: assimilationists, reactionaries, revisionists, and qualified separatists. His simulations have more in common with political theories in the literature of dominance than with the wild memories and rich diversities of tribal and postindian literature.

The novelists Pokagon, John Oskison, the author of *Wild Harvest*, *Black Davy*, and *Brothers Three*, and John Mathews, the author of *Sundown*, are classified as assimilationists because, it seems, some of the characters in their novels lean toward the literature of dominance. "Taken together," Larson wrote, these and other assimilationist novels are "conventional in form, traditional in subject, anything but innovative," and "indistinguishable from hundreds of other fic-

tional works of the time. . . . If we did not know that these men
were Native Americans we might conclude from their novels that
they were white."

Larson seemed to search for the romance of racial purities or the
antiselves in tribal literature because his four categories are denials
of crossblood identities and tribal survivance; he assumed, based on
the novels he considered, that he would discover and understand the
essential tribal experience. However, he dedicated more attention to
the colonial conditions of determining tribal identities and enroll-
ment documentation on reservations than to the criticism of racialism, the cruelties of relocation, the burdens of federal assimilation
policies, and manifest manners in commercial publishing.

"Suddenly he was dreaming," Mathews wrote in *Sundown*. Chal-
lenge Windzer "was riding at the end of a party of warriors, and the
Pawnees were fleeing over the hill before them, calling in Pawnee,
'Here comes Chal and his Osage Wolves.' He could see a white girl
standing there on the prairie in long blue mantle like the mantle of
the Virgin Mary, and she turned toward him as a savior. The reasons for her predicament were absent, but the dream was delightful.
When she tried to thank him he frowned and walked away, but his
dream-heart was full."

Owens observed that the "romantic atmosphere begins to disappear from the Indian novel in the 1930s with the appearance of fiction by Mathews" and D'Arcy McNickle. "Writing of the nightmare
time of new oil money and dissolution for the Osage, Mathews per-
meates his novel, *Sundown*, with a feeling of naturalistic despair as
the protagonist, Chal Windzer, slips into the deracinated no-Indian's-
land between Osage and white worlds. In spite of subtle invocation of
sacred geography and patterns out of the oral tradition, both of which
hint at continuity and survival, McNickle, like Mathews, reflects the
grimness of the Hemingway era of naturalism in his first novel, *The*

Surrounded. Like Chal Windzer, McNickle's protagonist Archilde Leon never has a chance within a civilization bent on turning Indians into Europeans."

Larson represented education as assimilation rather than survivance; his arrogance would embrace the simulations of savagism and slander postindian imagination. "Paradoxically," he asserted, "Pokagon, Oskison, and Mathews would not have written and published novels if they had not received the schooling they did and been assimilated (in their varying degrees) into the white man's world. And that, of course, is the crux of their dilemma. Their education took something away from them, yet their writing became a way of reconciling or exploring the problems of assimilation that each man met in his own distinct way."

Larson reviewed *Seven Arrows* by Hyemeyohsts Storm as a historical revisionist novel because it depicted survival and "aggressive confrontations" between tribal people and the dominant culture. He insisted that the issue of how representative a tribal author might be "to his people" is a question "best left to cultural anthropologists." Storm was denounced by some tribal elders for his personal interpretations of cultural traditions and for his pose as a member of the Northern Cheyenne. The paperbound edition of the novel was released over the objections of traditional tribal elders on the reservation. Such serious tribal matters are not the mission of anthropologists.

"Nothing that sets itself above the community escapes ridicule," wrote Terrence Des Pres in *Writing into the World.* He was dedicated to the literature of survivance and studied the absence of humor and satire in the stories of the Holocaust. "In its homage to fact, the mode of high seriousness has no option but to attempt convincing likeness. It's this 'realism,' this compulsion to reproduce exactly, that almost necessarily ensures defeat. Comic works, on the contrary, make no attempt to actual representation. Laughter, in this case, is hostile to the world it depicts. It is free as tragedy and lamentation are not." Des Pres pointed out that the horrors of human histories have to be treated with reverence in literature; this, a "tragic seriousness," and the absence of humor in the experiences of real destitution and the histories of massacres are conditions that would describe the solemn responses of those who write about reservations. Too often, there is a tragic flaw in reason, and the wisdom learned by chance and adversities is lost to seriousness and the "hegemony" of histories. The tribes are reduced to the tragic in the ruins of representation; tragic wisdom endures, and is the source of trickster humor in the literature of survivance, but the wisdom has been denied to conserve the tragic as a common theme in manifest manners and dominance. The tribes have seldom been honored for their trickster stories and rich humor. The resistance to tribal humor is a tragic flaw. Laughter over that comic touch in tribal stories would not steal the breath of destitute children; rather, children would be healed with humor, and manifest manners would be undermined at the same time.

"We presume to liberate the future by placing ourselves in bondage to the past," wrote Des Pres. "In the realm of art, a comic response is more resilient, more effective in revolt against terror and the sources of terror than a response that is solemn or tragic."

Larson pointed out that "in theory I believe that asking such questions is a futile exercise. In practice, however, some benefit may be derived from the answer simply because by and large we are dealing with ethnic materials that depict some aspect of the Indian-white confrontation. No doubt we would expect these writers to be true to the cultures they write about, though reading fiction solely to learn about another culture may be misleading. A novel must be something more than an anthropological document if it is to engage our aesthetic sensitivities."

Not to fault social science theories and the literature of dominance in the ruins of representation is to believe that the causes of racialism are the same as the simulations of manifest manners that pose as the cures. Larson noted that the tribal novelists he studied were educated, and their education, he assumed, was the end of tribal cultures. He must bear the tragic flaw of racial nihilism and melancholy; otherwise, he would mourn the ruinous simulations of dominance.

D'Arcy McNickle and N. Scott Momaday are categorized as reactionaries because their novels are about "individuals, isolated Indians trapped in the present world, unable to return to the ways of the past."

McNickle and Momaday are recognized as distinguished scholars in two worlds, and their publications, though separated by a generation, are related in theme. The central characters in their novels, Archilde in *The Surrounded* by McNickle, first published in 1936, and Abel in *House Made of Dawn* by Momaday, published in 1968, are crossbloods who returned to reservations; these characters return to memories, a memorable landscape, and their wretched families. "Although their present existence is individualistic, the past from which they have been severed is collective," wrote Larson. He asserted that Momaday, who won the Pulitzer Prize for *House Made of Dawn*, "has become trapped in a literary holding pattern. . . . With a vision as bleak as his, one wonders whether Momaday can write another novel about the Native American without making a complete reversal and thereby undermining the validity of his earlier work."

Larson was a hardhearted reader, to be sure, and his captious criticism was unwarranted then and now. "That night Grey dreamed of sleeping with a bear," Momaday wrote in *The Ancient Child*, his second novel. "The bear drew her into its massive arms and licked her body and her hair. It hunched over her, curving its spine like a cat, until its huge body seemed to have absorbed her own. Its breath, which bore a deep, guttural rhythm like language, touched her skin with low, persistent heat. The bear's tongue kneaded her—her feet, her belly and her breasts, her throat. Her own breathing became exaggerated, and there were long, orgasmic surges within her; she felt that her body was flooding with blood. The dream was full of wonder. . . .

"Set took the medicine bundle in his hands and opened it. The smell of it permeated the whole interior. When he drew on the great paw, there grew up in him a terrible restlessness, wholly urgent, and his heart began to race. He felt the power of the bear pervade his being, and the awful compulsion to release it. Grey, sitting away in the invisible dark, heard the grandmother's voice in her mouth. When Set raised the paw, as if to bring it down like a club, she saw it against the window, huge and phallic on the stars, each great yellow claw like the horn of the moon."

Larson praised *Winter in the Blood* by James Welch as an "almost flawless novel . . . one of the most significant pieces of fiction by an American Indian." Welch and Leslie Marmon Silko, the author of *Ceremony*, are named qualified separatists, the last category invented by Larson. The characters in these novels lived in urban areas and "survived because they adapted themselves to the dual world that surrounded them."

Silko and the characters in *Ceremony* are not separatists, no matter how clever the critical reviews and interpretations might sound in *American Indian Fiction*. LaVonne Ruoff is closer to the heart of *Ceremony*. She observed that Silko "demonstrates the healing power of tribal ritual and storytelling by reuniting her mixed-blood hero with his tribe at the end of the novel. More overtly than Momaday, she evokes myth and ritual."

"I have made changes in the rituals. The people mistrust this greatly, but only this growth keeps the ceremonies strong," said the crossblood healer Betonie in *Ceremony*. "They are things the witchery people want. Witchery works to scare people, to make them fear growth. But it has always been necessary, and more than ever now, it is. Otherwise we won't make it. We won't survive. That's what the witchery is counting on: that we will cling to the ceremonies the way they were, and then their power will triumph, and the people will be no more."

Several Native American Indian novelists have published, in the past decade, their own studies of tribal consciousness, culture, and literatures. Paula Gunn Allen, in *The Sacred Hoop*, overturned androcentric structuralism, praised spiritualism, and celebrated a renaissance of the feminine in postindian literatures. She boosted social and familial responsibilities and pointed out that one of the "major distinguishing characteristics of gynocratic cultures is the absence of punitiveness as a means of social control. Another is the inevitable presence of meaningful concourse with supernatural beings."

The notion that tribal thought is "mystical and psychic" by nature, and that there is a "presence" of "supernatural beings," is close to some of the observations, but not the gender dominance, in *How Natives Think* by Lucien Lévy-Bruhl, the nineteenth-century philosopher. Primitive man "lives and acts in an environment of beings and objects, all of which, in addition to the properties that we recognize them to possess, are endued with mystic attributes. He perceives their objective reality mingled with another reality. He feels himself surrounded by an infinity of imperceptible entities, nearly always invisible to sight, and always redoubtable," and at times the souls of the dead.

"Among gynocratic or gynocentric tribal people the welfare of the young is paramount," Allen observed. The "complementary nature of all life forms is stressed, and the centrality of powerful women to social well-being is unquestioned."

Allen avowed lesbian spiritualism as a postindian simulation, and she maintained that tribal "thought is essentially mystical and psychic in nature." She considered the ethics of essentialist tribal literature, or "using the tradition," in a conversation published in the *Headlands Journal*: "I have specialized in teaching contemporary literature to avoid as many ethical violations as I could, believing that I might teach it and evade or avoid queries about arcane matters." Moreover, "I have gone so far as to learn as little ritual or myth as possible in any particular detail to further buttress my defense against ethical violations. . . .

"I begin to understand some of the reasons for my extreme ambivalence in doing what I do, some of the reasons I find teaching in Native American Studies so painful, and some of the reasons why some of the poems and fiction I've been working on for years is stymied," she said in a discussion on the problems of teaching the novel *Ceremony* by Leslie Marmon Silko.

On the other hand, she pointed out that the preservation of tradition "with the sacrifice of its living bearers seems at best reasonless, at worst blasphemous. If people die as a result of preserving tradition in the white way of preservation, for whom will the tradition be preserved?"

Allen considered the obvious contradictions of essentialism and postindian crossblood identities in a personal and indicative comment in *The Sacred Hoop*: "For although I am a somewhat nontraditional Indian, I grew up in the homes of Indians and have spent my adult life in the company of traditionals, urbanites, and all the shades of Indian in between. . . .

"Whatever I read about Indians I check out with my inner self. Most of what I have read—and some things I have said based on that reading—is upside-down and backward. But my inner self, the self who knows what is true of American Indians because it *is* one, always warns me when something deceptive is going on. And with that warning, I am moved to do a great deal of reflecting, some more reading, and a lot of questioning and observing of real live human beings who are Indian in order to discover the source of my unease. Sometimes that confirmation comes about in miraculous ways; that's when I know guidance from the nonphysicals and the supernaturals, and that the Grandmothers have taken pity on me in my dilemma."

Elizabeth Cook-Lynn is the founder and editor of the *Wicazo Sa Review*. She has published interpretations, critical studies, and reviews that sustain tribal values and governments. Her recent novel, *From the River's Edge*, celebrates the honorable conditions of tribal sovereignty and survivance.

Cook-Lynn, in a critical commentary on *Sending My Heart Back Across the Years* by Hertha Dawn Wong, wrote that the "wannabee sentiment which clutters an otherwise tolerable piece of redundant scholarship is a reflection of a growing phenomenon which precedes and influences the intellectual discourse now emerging from universities all over the place in the name of Native American Studies." Moreover, she argued, the "unnecessary claim of this scholar to be 'part Native American' is so absurd as to cast ridicule on the work itself. But, more seriously, the 'blood quantum' debate, the '*ethnic identity*' issue, has finally obscured or dismissed one of the important sovereign rights of Indian nations, and neither Congress nor the Supreme Court had to act in its usual dubious ways." She pointed out with a sense of ironic humor that curriculum development at universities "has been reduced to offerings which might be called 'What If I'm a Little Bit Indian?' "

Narrative Chance: Postmodern Discourse on Native American Literatures was the first collection of essays on the postmodern condition in tribal literatures and poststructural interpretations of tribal cultures and consciousness. Alan Velie pointed out in an essay that since "the trickster is the most important mythic figure in most tribes it is not surprising that he would be a major archetype in contemporary Indian fiction. Quite a few protagonists in recent Indian novels bear a resemblance to the trickster." I argued in my essay that "the trickster is androgynous, a comic healer and liberator in literature; the *whole figuration* that ties the unconscious to social experience. The trickster sign is communal, an erotic shimmer in oral traditions; the narrative voices are *holotropes* in a discourse."

Louis Owens has published the most recent critical studies of Native American Indian novelists. *Other Destinies: Understanding the American Indian Novel* is the third title in the new American Indian Literature and Critical Studies series at the University of Oklahoma Press. Owens considered the themes of cultural survival, the interpretations and recoveries of tribal identities in the characters and scenes created by mixedblood novelists. His second novel, *The Sharpest Sight*, is the first title in the new literature series.

Owens pointed out that *The Surrounded* by D'Arcy McNickle was first entitled "The Hungry Generations," a "version almost twice as long as the published manuscript, and very different in its implications." Archilde, the protagonist, in the earlier version is "allowed to travel to Paris and to experience the heady atmosphere" and milieu of the Lost Generation. He falls in love and returns to Montana. Harcourt, Brace and Company returned "The Hungry Generations" on April 6, 1929, with a rejection letter that said the story of an Indian "wandering between two generations, two cultures," was excellent. "A new territory to be explored: ancient material used for a different end. Perhaps the beginning of a new Indian literature to rival that of Harlem." *The Surrounded* was published seven years later.

"The distinctions between the two versions might well be compared to that between a conventional romance and a naturalistic novel," wrote Owens. "In the former much confusion of identity and potential disaster lead to marriage and the promise of a fruitful future; chaos is ordered and controlled. In the latter, the protagonist simply cannot understand much less order and control the world he inhabits. The question of who he is remains unanswered." These are distinctions between the manifest manners of dominance and the simulations of survivance. The first version of the novel was a story of survivance; the published novel is a tragic closure without the wisdom of tribal experiences.

"What it boils down to is respecting your world, every little piece of it. When I poach does at night, it's against the law," said Hoey in *The Sharpest Sight*. "But what I'm doing ain't wrong if you look at it in an Indian way. I pick out old does past their prime. . . . And I leave the best breeding bucks and does alone. That ain't like the poison that chicken plant dumps into the creek, the stuff that kills the fish, or all the rest of things people are doing to the earth."

Maydean Joe and Harlen Bigbear are comic characters in *Medicine River* by Thomas King. Harlen "was like the prairie wind. You never knew when he was coming or when he was going to leave." Maydean was backward, tenacious, and a trickster silhouette in the literature of survivance.

"Maydean Joe was retarded. She lived in the apartment building next door to ours, and every so often," said the narrator, she "would wander into our basement. . . . Henry Goodrider told her it was our basement, and that if she wanted to play in it, she would have to pay."

The boys played tricks on her in the basement. "She fell down, and then she got up and pushed Henry, and Henry pushed her back, and then she pushed me. We all started pushing each other, and then we started laughing, and after that, Maydean was okay."

"I don't mean she got better or anything like that. She was still retarded. She liked to hug us, and that was embarrassing . . . She was strong, and she liked to squeeze us as hard as she could." Other kids teased her, called her names and drew pictures of her on the wall.

"One day, she sort of went wild in the basement and started scrubbing at a picture Vicki had drawn. Maydean tried to erase it with her bare hands, and she got most of it off, but not before she cut her hands on the concrete. They didn't bleed much, but you could see the faint fan of blood on the wall."

Maydean is a postindian conversion, an eminent trickster silhouette that overturns mannish manners in a conventional basement. The other characters are comic, to be sure, but the ironic caution of the narrator bears no tribal visions. The narrator without a vision is a trickster simulation without a tribal shadow.

"It was Henry's idea that we put Maydean in the dryer," but she "was stubborn sometimes, and this was one of those times. So we were stuck with James." He bounced around and bloodied his nose. "Maydean's fault," said Henry. "She was supposed to do it, but she didn't want to because she's crazy."

Diane Glancy created ironic silhouettes in *Firesticks*, a collection of stories. The narrator is a sober attestor of tribal manners and memories at a curious distance. The shadows of humor are elusive, and the avows concise. "Now this is what I have against Indians. I don't think they care for the land they say they care for. I think they're irresponsible. They only care about their good times. High hooters. Rooty fluters. Ghosters. Who thought they could call back buffalo. Thought they could return the ancestors. Handle firewater. . . . Oh I know, be generous. Their culture was ripped off, then they're expected to be kind to the earth. We expect them to do more with less."

The narrator was not "a card-carrying Indian. Not a card-carrying White. But schoolteacher, provider, minority, and everything nobody else wanted to be. An Indian because I wasn't White. An Indian because I could synthesize the fragments and live with hurt. Yipes."

LaVonne Ruoff is the undeniable leader of serious research and education in tribal literatures, and she is the most admired historical interpreter of contemporary novels and poetry. "The history of American Indian literature reflects not only tribal cultures and the experience of imagination of its authors but Indian-white relations as well," she wrote in *American Indian Literatures*. "Although individual Indians today vary in the extent to which they follow tribal traditions, their worldviews and values continue to reflect those of their ancestors."

A Son of the Forest by William Apess, published in 1829, may be the first autobiography by a tribal person and distinct from those "autobiographies" of Indians written by others. Ruoff pointed out that Apess was an orphan and that the "whites" Apess lived with as a child "taught him to be terrified of his own people. If he disobeyed, they threatened to punish him by sending him to the forest."

Apess was crossblood Pequot, a Methodist minister, and an activist for tribal rights. "His own birth and death are not documented," Barry O'Connell observed in *On Our Own Ground*. "Born to a nation despised and outcast and perhaps, to add to the stigma, not only part white, a 'mulatto' or 'mixed breed,' but also part African American, a child with William Apess's history who simply made it to adulthood would be doing well." The once despised other learned how to write his name and stories over the racial borders in a crossblood remembrance.

"I cannot perhaps give a better idea of the dread which pervaded my mind on seeing any of my brethren of the forest than by relating the following occurrence," Apess wrote in his autobiography. "One day several of the family went into the woods to gather berries, taking me with them. We had not been out long before we fell in with a company of white females, on the same errand—their complexion was, to say the least, as *dark* as that of the natives. The circumstance filled my mind with terror, and I broke from the party with my utmost speed, and I could not muster courage enough to look behind until I had reached home," wrote Apess. "It may be proper for me here to remark that the great fear I entertained of my brethren was occasioned by the many stories I had heard of their cruelty toward the whites. . . . If the whites had told me how cruel they had been to the 'poor Indian,' I should have apprehended as much harm from them."

Tribal autobiographical narratives and personal life stories have been popular for more than a century. George Copway and Sarah Winnemucca both published autobiographies in the nineteenth century. Charles Eastman, Francis La Flesche, Luther Standing Bear, and John Joseph Mathews published their autobiographies and personal narratives in the early twentieth century.

Standing Bear was raised a century ago to be a hunter and warrior, but the federal government had terminated the buffalo and he was removed to be educated at the government school at Carlisle, Pennsylvania. He wrote that when "the train stopped at the station" in Sioux City, "we raised the windows to look out" and "there was a great crowd of white people there." The white people "started to throw money at us. We little fellows began to gather up the money, but the larger boys told us not to take it, but to throw it back at them."

The Names, by N. Scott Momaday, is a memoir of stories on a landscape of silence and shadows. "My spirit was quiet there," he wrote about his childhood at Jemez, New Mexico. "The silence was old, immediate, and pervasive, and there was great good in it. The wind of the canyons drew it out; the voices of the village carried and were lost in it. Much was made of the silence; much of the summer and winter was made of it."

I Tell You Now: Autobiographical Essays by Native American Writers, edited by Brian Swann and Arnold Krupat, includes literary autobiographies by Maurice Kenny, Elizabeth Cook-Lynn, Carter Revard, Jack Forbes, Paula Gunn Allen, Diane Glancy, Simon Ortiz, Linda Hogan, Joy Harjo, and nine other writers.

Elizabeth Cook-Lynn was born in the Government Hospital at Fort Thompson, South Dakota. She remembers silence, mistrust of the world, and then anger. "That anger is what started me writing. Writing, for me, then, is an act of defiance born of the need to survive. I am me. I exist. I am a Dakotah," she wrote. "It is an act of courage, I think. And, in the end, as Simon Ortiz says, it is an act that defies oppression.

"In those early days, even though I had a need to write—that is, to survive—I lived in a world in which the need to write was not primary. The need 'to tell,' however, was. And so I listened and heard about a world that existed in the flesh and in the imagination, too, and in the hearts and minds of real people. In those days I thought the world was made up of 'Siouxs' and 'Wasichus.' "

Maurice Kenny was born in northern New York state near the foothills of the Adirondacks. He was a shy child of Mohawk ancestry. "I have hunted not only words and images, metaphors, but, to my mother's relish, also song," he wrote in *I Tell You Now*. "I have heard the cedar sing, I have listened to the white pine, I have imitated white-tail deer and hawk and cocked an ear even to the more plain song of robin, a running brook, chicory weaving on summer winds. I have sung the round dance of the Longhouse—feet stomping the wooden floor, drum beating, singers' throats throbbing."

Jim Barnes is of Choctaw and Welsh ancestry. "I was five years old the last time I heard the mountain lion scream. That was in Oklahoma, 1938, when times were hard and life was good—and sacred," he wrote in his autobiographical essay. "But a year later the WPA had done its work: roads were cut, burial mounds were dug, small concrete dams were blocking nearly every stream. The Government was caring for its people. Many were the make-work jobs. A man could eat again, while all about him the land suffered. The annual spring migration of that lone panther was no more. The riverbanks that had been his roads and way stations bore the scars of the times, the scars of loss.

"In my mind the rivers must always run free. But in truth today I do not recognize them. They are alien bodies on a flattening land where everything has been made safe, civilized into near extinction. Sounds of speedboats drown out the call of the remaining jays and crows. The din of highway traffic carries for miles now that the timber has fallen to chainsaw or chemical rot. Green silence in the heavy heat of summer afternoons is no more."

"When I was about nine my family moved into a northern sec-
tion of Los Angeles, and there I would have psychologically perished
had it not been for a range of hills that came up to our back yard,"
wrote Jack Forbes. "The hills were full of animals—deer, snakes,
coyotes, birds—and I spent much of my spare time crawling along
deer trails through brush and exploring draws and canyons. In one
nearby canyon was a giant oak tree, and under its branches, where
they brushed against the top of a sharp rise in the canyon wall, I had
one of my favorite hiding places. Like an animal of the earth, I loved
to rest in such secret places, where I could see but not be seen, and
where I could dream."

Native American Indian authors have secured the rich memories
of tribal generations on this continent; the diverse narratives of these
crossblood authors would uncover the creative humor of survivance
and tribal counterpoise to the literature of dominance. These autobiographical essays would overcome the racialism of discoveries and
the romanticism of tribal cultures.

"This conscious awareness of the singularity of each individual
life is the late product of a specific civilization," wrote Georges Gus-
dorf in *Autobiography*, edited by James Olney. "Throughout most of
human history, the individual does not oppose himself to all others;
he does not feel himself to exist outside of others, and still less against
others, but very much *with* others in an independent existence that
asserts its rhythms everywhere in the community. No one is rightful
possessor of his life or his death; lives are so thoroughly entangled
that each of them has its center everywhere and its circumference
nowhere."

These theories and critical notions, with certain conditions, are the
most common interpretations of literary autobiographies by tribal
writers. In other words, the common conceit is that an autobiographer must "oppose himself to all others," or oppose tribal cultures
and reservation communities. Such notions are romantic at least, and

nurture the whimsies of savagism and otherness at best. The suspicion seems to be that there are communal representations, but not universal, and memories that cannot be heard in certain pronouns; the translations of unheard pronouns have never been the sources of tribal or postindian consciousness.

The favors of certain pronouns, however, are not the same in translation or tribal autobiographies: pronouns are neither the sources, causes, nor tribal intentions; autobiographies, memories, and personal stories are not the authentic representations of either pronouns, cultures, or the environment.

The stories that are heard are the coherent memories of natural reason; the stories that are read are silent landscapes. Pronouns, then, are the pinch hitters in the silence and distance of translation, and at the same time pronouns are the *différance* that would be unheard in translations. The shadows of tribal consciousness, and the shadows of names and natural reason are overheard in tribal stories and autobiographies; in this sense, stories are shadows, shimmers of coincidence, and tribal traceries in translation. The shadows are unsure scenes in dreams with bears, birds, and demons, and the *différance*, or temporization of pronouns, in tribal nicknames, memories, dance moves, and shamanic visions.

Swann and Krupat, for instance, pointed out in the introduction to *I Tell You Now* that "the notion of telling the whole of any one individual's life or taking merely personal experience as of particular significance was, in the most literal way, foreign to them, if not also repugnant."

The concerted simulations of tribal cultures are in continuous translations, and the situation of hermeneutics remains the same in simulations; the silence of translation and the absence of the heard antecedes a presence and the shadows of stories. Has the absence of the heard in tribal memories and stories become the literature of dominance? What are the real names, nouns, and pronouns heard in the unbearable simulations of tribal consciousness? How can a pronoun be a source of tribal identities in translation? How can a pronoun be a representation, an inscription of absence, a simulation of the presence of sound, and a person in translation?

The first person pronoun has never been the original absence of the heard, not even as the absence or transvaluation in the silence of a reader. The unheard presence of pronouns, and the temporization of nouns, is the *différance* heard in tribal nicknames and in the absence of the heard in translations. Certain tribal nicknames are stories, and the stories are distinctions that would counter the notions of communal memories. The survivance of tribal nicknames, shadows, and memories, in the absence of the heard, is the *différance* that misconstrues the representations of presence, simulations, and the gender burdens of pronouns. The personal, possessive, demonstrative, relative, and interrogative pronouns are translations and transvaluations, the absence of names, presence, and consciousness heard in tribal stories.

The pronoun endures as twice the absence of the heard, and more than the mere surrogate signifier or simulation in tribal stories. There is a sense of the heard in the absence of the heard; the pronoun is the *différance* that would pronounce and misconstrue memories in postindian literature. We must represent our own pronoun poses in autobiographies, in our personal invitations to silence and shadows of the heard; first person pronouns have no referent. The other is a continuous pronoun with no shadows, the pronominal simulation of antiselves. The demonstrative pronouns are the transactions of others, the elusive invitations to a presence in the absence of postindian entities.

We must need new pronouns that would misconstrue gender binaries, that would combine the want of a presence in the absence of the heard, a shadow pronoun to pronounce remembrance in silence, in the absence of postindian names, nouns, and deverbatives. The *pro-*

nounance combines the sense of the words *pronoun* and *pronounce* with the actions and conditions of survivance in tribal memories and stories. The *pronounance* of trickster hermeneutics has a shadow with no person, time, or number. In the absence of the heard the trickster is the shadow of the name, the sound, the noun, the person, the *pronounance*.

The tribal healers, shamanic visionaries, and those who hear stories in the blood are not bound to measure their memories as the mere hurrah for nature. Tribal landscapes are heard, read, and the scenes and shadows are remembered in stories. The coherence of natural reason is created in personal stories, and in the elusive unions of shamans with birds, animals, and ancestors. These natural unions are heard in the shadows that outlast translations. The shamans hear their memories in birds, animals, and shadows in our stories.

The theories of structuralism, the myths of the universal and unexpected harmonies, and objective dissociations of natural tribal reason are dubious tropes to power in the literature of dominance. The simulations of manifest manners, causal evidence, objectivism, and transitive action have no referent, no sense of postindian play in language and experience, no shadows in silence, and no coherence of natural reason. The tribal referent is in the shadows of heard stories; shadows are their own referent, and shadows are the silence and simulations of survivance.

Those lonesome souls who must read their identities in metanarratives and trace the distance of their tribal ancestors to an environment of otherness in the literature of dominance are the new missionaries of simulations. The identities that arise from simulations of the environment have no referent or shadow in tribal or postindian consciousness. "Since the environment cannot be authentically engaged the self becomes its own environment and sole source of authenticity," John Aldridge wrote in *The American Novel and the Way We Live Now*, "while all else becomes abstract and alien."

Hertha Dawn Wong, for instance, declared in the preface to *Sending My Heart Back Across the Years* that she is "not a member of a native community, but much of what my mother taught me reflects traditional values long associated with Native American cultures." No doubt she heard the memorable simulations of a tribal environment. Nonetheless, she must be held to her own high academic standards of historical and theoretical research on tribal literature.

Wong has studied Native American autobiographies; at the same time, she seems to praise panoramic tribal identities and a romantic narrative environment. "Over the years," she wrote, "the unfolding narrative of my family history and the narrative of this book on autobiography have taken on striking parallels."

The narratives she studied in *Sending My Heart Back Across the Years* could be considered the elusive sources of her own sense of postindian identities; otherwise, the overture to the "fundamental activities of autobiography" would be insincere invitations to these associations. The rights and duties of tribal consciousness have never been established in tribal communities or, for that matter, in the literature of dominance; imagination is an honorable performance, but autobiographies must arise from memories and the shadows of heard stories. Neither the first person nor the indirect reflexive pronoun are reasonable sources of identities; notions of tribal romanticism and metaphorical parallelism are earnest but without assurance. The subject of her research has become the object of her tribal identities; alas, tribal memories were never heard in objectivism or the simulations of manifest manners.

"When I began writing this book," she wrote in the preface, "I had little idea that I was part Native American, one of the unidentified mixed-bloods whose forebears wandered away from their fractured communities, leaving little cultural trace in their adopted world." The racialism of these romantic notions would bear minimal honor in tribal memories and literature.

Wong musters the innocence of a wanderer in the simulation of a postindian crossblood, and she poses in a transitive narrative on tribal cultures; the metaphor of adoption serves the literature of dominance. "I found a new insight into the meaning of irony," she wrote. "I had believed that I was a non-Indian writing as an outsider about Native American autobiographical traditions."

The conceit of innocuous environmental identities must be ironic, because the panoramic other is a romantic transvaluation and simulation, a consumer precedence over the coherence of natural reason. *Sending My Heart Back Across the Years* could be read as ironic and impressionistic criticism in the literature of dominance.

"My purpose is to expand the Eurocentric definitions of autobiography to include nonwritten forms of personal narratives," she wrote in the introduction. "This study, then, considers Native American autobiography from the context of autobiographical theory, delineates distinctly Native American oral and pictographic traditions of personal narrative and their interaction with Euro-American autobiographical modes." Moreover, she argues that both "female and Native American autobiographical narratives focus on a communal or relational identity and tend to be cyclical rather than linear." How, then, could she have overlooked the significant studies of *pictomyths*, or picture stories, and tribal music at the turn of the last century by Frances Densmore?

Wong widens the serious textual discourse on autobiographies, to be sure, but her earnest search for communalism is closer to an absolute literature than to the nuances of tribal identities. The pictures she construes as autobiographies are picture myths, stories, or memorial expressionism, not historical representations. Tribal narratives are heard and remembered in *pictofiction* and *pictomyths* without closure.

Wong declared that there "is no generic Indian sense of self." Indeed, and that assertion could be read as the closure of her own panoramic sense of tribal identities in literature. "If a Native American sense of self is associated with tribal identity, to realize fully a sense of Indian identity is to realize one's link to the tribe." True, the "concept of 'race' or 'ethnic origins' means different things in different contexts," wrote Douglas Benson and John Hughes in *Ethnomethodology*. However, when the tropes to academic power are tied to the simulations of nativism and tribal identities, then the context of racialism is prescribed as both essentialist and political in institutions.

The racialism that surrounded the documentation of the tribal descent of individuals, reservation residence, and the obscure measures of bloom quantums was driven by tedious bureaucracies. Government attention has turned from the blood quantum of each tribal person recorded on a reservation to natural resources, casinos, and reservation economies; even so, the notion of an arithmetic reduction of blood as a historical document is no less detestable and detrimental to mental health.

The Indian Agents who wrote to the Commissioner of Indian Affairs, for instance, about a reservation relocation petition indicate the absurd federal tolerance over the trivial details of domination on reservations. The Indian Agent at the Crow Agency in Montana wrote on 2 March 1901 to explain that he had received a petition that E. C. Means of Pine Ridge, South Dakota, "be transfered with his brothers George W., Robert B., Frank, and Charles Means to this Agency, which enclosure contains the statement that their mother was full-blooded Crow Indian and that they are half-breeds and have been erroneously enrolled with the Pine Ridge Sioux." Four months later the Crow Indian Council agreed to their return to the Crow reservation in Montana.

The Indian Agent at the Crow Agency wrote once more to the Commissioner of Indian Affairs in Washington on 4 September 1901 that the Crow Indians met in council on the Little Horn, and that "the following was given to me as facts in the matter by the chief of this tribe 'Pretty Eagle' and corroborated by all the members of the tribe present, from say forty years of age up: 'That about the year 1872 the mother of the Means brothers with her sister went from this tribe with soldiers to Fort Laramie, Wyoming; that in the year 1888 she returned to the Crow tribe having left five sons by a white man for their father on the Pine Ridge Reservation. She died some four years later. The sister never returned to her own tribe. The mother's relatives are 'Shot in the Arm,' 'Spotted Horse' and 'Plain Owl Brothers.' Each of the latter made the above statement. The younger men of the tribe stated that they were not born or were too young to know of this and said, 'If you, the Agent, think they should return we have no objection.' "

These letters, written by government agents and copied from a federal archive five generations later, are the sources of stories about tribal names and interests on reservations. The letters, and other documents, can be important sources of tribal histories, of course; these documents are also critical sources of information about the histories of reservation families and the burdens of reservation residence. Such trivial documentation is the literature of domination; at the same time, the obvious burdens of reservation residence in the past could become valuable evidence in the histories of tribal families.

Anthony Kerby argued in *Narrative and the Self* that "for much of our lives a concern with self-identity may be marginal at best. Questions of identity and self-understanding arise primarily in crisis situations and at certain turning points in our routine behavior. Such events often call for self-appraisal. That we have, at any moment, the *belief* in a continuous and relatively unchanging identity is itself little more than one story we have learned to tell ourselves." He continued, "in other words, in narrating the past we understand ourselves to be the implied subject generated by the narrative." The "self is to be construed not as a prelinguistic given that merely employs language, much as we might employ a tool, but rather as a product of language—what might be called the *implied subject* of self-referring utterances."

The narrative selves, and the simulations of the antiselves, that have no referent, memories, or shadows, are the transitive selves overheard in language and literature; tribal shadows are intransitive and wait to be heard in stories. "Life does not speak; it listens and waits," wrote Gilles Deleuze and Félix Guattari in *A Thousand Plateaus*. "Language is not life; it gives life orders." Literature is the overheard other in the search for selves. Mikhail Bakhtin created the idea of heteroglossia, or the diversities of language, to consider the utterances of selves in the interaction of the other. "Words belong to nobody, and in themselves they evaluate nothing," he wrote in *Speech Genres and Other Late Essays*. "The *I* hides in the other and in others, it wants to be only an other for others, to enter completely into the word of others as an other, and to cast from itself the burden of being the only *I* (*I-for-myself*) in the world."

On the other hand, the confessions, simulations of transitive antiselves, and panoramic identities could be an ironic liberation of pronouns in the literature of dominance. Francis Jacques points out in *Difference and Subjectivity* that the first person singular pronoun "is not knowable because it knows. No objectivization, no representation of the subjective in this sense is possible, since any representation is objective. . . . But even if I cannot know this *I*, I can still be conscious of it."

Anthony Kenny was uncertain about the stature and sense of pronouns in sentences. "If 'I' is not a proper name shall we simply say then that it is a pronoun? The grammatical category of pronouns is a ragbag, including even variables," he wrote in "The First Person," published in *Intention and Intentionality*. The "suggestion given by the word's etymology that it can be replaced by a noun in a sentence while preserving the sense of the sentence, is false of 'I.' Shall we say that 'I' is a demonstrative?" The first person pronoun that bears the stories in autobiographies must be the absence of the subject; the noun, the name, is superseded by the simulation of the pronoun in a sentence that would be the *implied subject* of the narrative; implied subjects, then, are *implied identities* in the literature of dominance.

The pleasure of nicknames in tribal memories is an unmistakable sign and celebration of personal identities; nicknames are personal stories that would, to be sure, trace the individual in tribal families and communities rather than cause separations by personal recognition. Even so, nicknames and stories change, a condition that liberates personal identities from the melancholy of permanence.

There is nothing foreign or repugnant in personal names and the stories that arise from nicknames. Sacred names and nicknames were heard as stories, and there were relatives and others responsible for giving names in most tribal communities. The signatures and traces of tribal names are heard in stories. The risks, natural reason, shadows, and pleasures of dreams and visions are sources of personal power in tribal consciousness; personal stories are coherent and name individual identities within tribal communities, and are not an obvious postindian opposition to communal values.

Personal visions, for instance, were heard alone, but not in cultural isolation or separation from tribal communities. Those who chose to hear visions were aware that their creative encounters with the unknown were precarious and would be sanctioned by the tribe; personal visions could be of service to tribal families and communities. Some personal visions and stories have the power to liberate and heal, and there are similar encounters that liberate readers in the novels and poems by contemporary postindian authors.

Nicknames, dreams, and shamanic visions are tribal stories that are heard and remembered as survivance. These personal stories are not the same as the literature of silence and dominance; these stories are not the same as translation and representational autobiographies. However, the awareness of coincidence in stories is much more sophisticated in tribal memories than in the tragic flaws of a consumer culture, and even wiser are the tribal memories that endured the colonial discoveries of antiselves and the cruelties of a chemical civilization.

Wovoka, the inspiration of the Ghost Dance religion, received many letters from tribal people who had heard about his vision in the very language of the treacherous colonial government. Luther Standing Bear, for instance, and thousands of other tribal men and women learned the language and literature of dominance; their memories and survivance were heard and read in more than one language.

Cloud Man Horse wrote to Wovoka, "Now I am going to send you a pair of mocissions but if they are not long enough for you when you write again please send me you foot measure from this day on—I will try to get the money to send to you. I wish I had it just at present I would sent it wright away."

The English language has been the linear tongue of colonial discoveries, racial cruelties, invented names, the simulation of tribal cultures, manifest manners, and the unheard literature of dominance in tribal communities; at the same time, this mother tongue of paracolonialism has been a language of invincible imagination and liberation for many tribal people in the postindian world. English, a language of paradoxes, learned under duress by tribal people at mission and federal schools, was one of the languages that carried the vision and shadows of the Ghost Dance, the religion of renewal, from tribe to tribe on the vast plains at the end of the nineteenth century. "The great underlying principle of the Ghost Dance doctrine is that the time will come when the whole Indian race, living and dead, will be reunited upon a regenerated earth, to live a life of aboriginal happiness, forever free from death, disease, and misery," wrote James Mooney in *The Ghost-Dance Religion*.

Captain Dick, a Paiute, said that "Indians who don't dance, who don't believe in this word," of the Ghost Dance, "will grow little, just about a foot high, and stay that way. Some of them will be turned into wood and be burned in the fire."

English, that coercive language of federal boarding schools, has carried some of the best stories of endurance, the shadows of tribal survivance, and now that same language of dominance bears the creative literature of distinguished postindian authors in the cities. The tribal characters dance with tricksters, birds, and animals, a stature that would trace the natural reason, coherent memories, transformations, and shadows in traditional stories. The shadows and language of tribal poets and novelists could be the new ghost dance literature, the shadow literature of liberation that enlivens tribal survivance.

ETERNAL HAVENS

The Admiral of the Ocean Sea was no trickster, but his return in the stories of children and ironic literature is cause to consider the wisdom of trickster hermeneutics and the simulations of survivance.

Christopher Columbus was the wounded adventurer, that third person discoverer of mother earth, and the absence of the real in the simulations of his name. Simulations are eternal havens, and he endures as the pronouns in trickster stories. He is the deverbative trickster, the one who landed in two pronouns, the he and you; the understudies of mother earth in the literature of discoveries.

Consider the second person, *you* are the trickster discoverer, and *you* land at dawn with no missionaries or naturalists; *you* hear the salamanders and rush of shamans. "No sooner had *you* concluded the formalities of taking possession of the island than people began to come to the beach," *you* wrote on October 12, 1492, at Samana Cay.

You are the discoverer of histories; you are the pronouns, the absence of the nouns in simulations, but not the redeemer. You are the deverbative reader, and you are the trickster hermeneutics in the tribal literature of survivance. The avowed discoveries land in the simulations of mother earth and the stories of children.

"Children don't read to find their identity," said Isaac Bashevis Singer when he accepted the National Book Award. Children "don't expect their beloved writer to redeem humanity. Young as they are, they know that it is not in his power. Only the adults have such childish illusions."

The *Santa Maria* was the best chance the children had to read and be named in the histories of a constitutional democracy. You land and discover marvelous shamans, tribal cultures with crystals, wild rice, and casinos. You discover mother earth and the eternal havens of simulations.

"In order to win their friendship, since *you* knew they were a people to be converted and won to our holy faith by love and friendship rather than by force, *you* gave them red caps and glass beads which they hung around their necks," you wrote in the journal. You are the discoverer in trickster hermeneutics.

Two men with the same surnames discovered two dimensions of the same obscure universe; curious, covetous, and possessed by their missions, both of these men discovered mother earth and the marvelous others. One discovered the internal penis, and the other bore the eternal penis.

Renaldus Columbus succeeded Andreas Vesalius as lecturer in surgery at the University of Padua. Columbus claimed that he discovered the clitoris, and the internal penis. Thomas Laqueur wrote in *Making Sex* that he was a "conquistador in an unknown land."

Christopher Columbus discovered the eternal haven of simulations; he landed in resistance literature. He heard no solace in tribal memories, no honor in the curia. His adventures have been espied more than tragic wisdom and the ecstasies of the shamans, and he has been honored in the stories of children over the tribal communities that were enslaved and terminated in his name.

Columbus was denied beatification because of his avarice, conceit, and the malevolence of his discoveries; nonetheless, several centuries later his missions and eternal stare were uncovered anew and commemorated as entitlements in a constitutional democracy.

The 1893 Columbian Exposition in Chicago, for instance, celebrated his discoveries as an enviable beat in the heart of the nation. Antonin Dvořák composed his occasional symphony *From the New World*. Cyrus Dallin, the sculptor, created *The Signal of Peace*, an equestrian tribal statue, and earned a medal at the Exposition, three years after the massacre at Wounded Knee. The bronze sculpture was honored more than tribal cultures; later, the statue was purchased for the city and dedicated in Lincoln Park. At the same time the federal government issued a memorial coin on the quadricentennial with an incuse of Columbus on one side and "the *Santa Maria* on the reverse." A similar commemorative coin has been struck for the quincentenary, and a "certificate of authenticity," as if there were gainsaid simulations, was issued with the purchase of each coin.

"The history of Native Americans only became useful when cultural resistance to Europe began to be important," wrote Michael Kammen in *Mystic Chords of Memory*. "Real Indians had largely disappeared by then from the mainstream view; so their legends could be approvingly used for aesthetic and symbolic motifs, as Dallin did, and to promote tourism. As *The Independent* remarked with open cynicism in 1903: 'Good Indian legends can be grown in almost any locality with a little care and attention.' During the 1890s ethnographers and anthropologists issued more frequent appeals that Indian myths and traditions be collected." Tribal ruins would become more significant in the nation, and each simulation of ancient histories was ironic, the undeniable absence of the tribes in the ruins of representation.

"The Spaniards were unable to exterminate the Indian race by those unparalleled atrocities which brand them with indelible shame, nor did they even succeed in wholly depriving it of its rights," wrote Alexis de Tocqueville in *Democracy in America*, "but the Americans of the United States have accomplished this twofold purpose with singular felicity; tranquilly, legally, philanthropically, without shedding blood, and without violating a single great principle of morality in the eyes of the world. It is impossible to destroy men with more respect for the laws of humanity."

Columbus is a miraculous representation of the nation, and he is a simulation of the long gaze of colonialism, that striven mannish stare with no salvation in the absence of the real. Indeed, the quincentenary is a double entendre, the long gaze celebration of colonial civilization in his names, and the discoveries of his name in a constitutional democracy. The want of humor must cause melancholy and a vague nostalgia for lost monarchies.

"Representation is miraculous because it deceives us into thinking it is realistic," wrote David Freedberg in *The Power of Images*, "but it is only miraculous because it is something other than what it represents."

The Dominican Republic commissioned an enormous and expensive quincentenary monument to celebrate the long gaze of the Admiral of the Ocean Sea. The *El Faro a Colón* "is equipped with lights that can project the shape of a cross high into the clouds" over the slums of Santa Domingo, reported the *Sunday Times* of London.

"Despite criticism that such extravagance is incompatible with the country's grim economic predicament," the blind, octogenarian president Joanquin Balaguer said, "the people need shoes but they also need a tie." Columbus is a commemorative curse not a communal tie; his names are the same as disease and death in the memories of the tribes on the island.

The Spaniards first landed on Hispaniola, wrote Bartolomé de Las Casas in *The Devastation of the Indies*. "Here those Christians perpetrated their first ravages and oppressions against the native peoples. This was the first land in the New World to be destroyed and depopulated by the Christians, and here they began their subjection of the women and children, taking them away from the Indians to use them and ill use them, eating the food they provided with their sweat and toil." The long colonial gaze is now a cross in the clouds, a remembrance of colonial cruelties and death.

The Government of the Bahamas issued a dollar note to commemorate the unmeant ironies of colonialism in the name of Christopher Columbus. The narrow gaze simulation of the adventurer on the souvenir note is based on a portrait by the Florentine painter Ridolfo Ghirlandaio.

"The long gaze fetishizes," observed David Freedberg, "and so too, unequivocally, does the handling of the object that signifies. All lingering over what is not the body itself, or plain understanding, is the attempt to eroticize that which is not replete with meaning." Columbus is the national fetish of discoveries.

Francis Parkman observed in *Pioneers of France in the New World* the claims that America "was found by Frenchmen." The word found, to come upon by accident, seems to be more accurate than discovered; that a nation was found is ironic, passive, and the simulation of lost continents. How could a new nation recover the found, or in a nautical note, "find one's bearings," four years before Christopher Columbus?

"This vast territory was claimed by Spain in right of the discoveries of Columbus, the grant of the Pope," and various other causes and conditions, wrote Parkman. "England claimed it in right of the discoveries of Cabot; while France could advance no better title than might be derived from the voyage of Verazzano and vague traditions of earlier visits by Breton adventures."

Parkman would sooner turn an ear to the ironies of historical ports of call, or lost and found discoveries, than consider the real miseries of the tribes under trinary colonial claims. "America, when it became known to Europeans, was, as it has long been, a scene of wide-spread revolution," he wrote in *The Jesuits in North America*. The "Indian,

hopelessly unchanging in respect to individual and social development, was, as regarded tribal relations and local haunts, mutable as
the wind."

Native American Indians have endured the historical ironies over
lost and found discoveries, the rights of treasures, and continental encounters for more than twenty generations. The tribes, however, are
not the only cultures to resist the discoveries of Columbus. Michael
Kammen, in *Mystic Cords of Memory*, wrote that a newspaper editorial at the turn of the last century argued nobody needs a holiday
to think about the discovery of America, nobody but "our engaging
friends of the Mafia would need all day in which to celebrate the feat
of their compatriot."

Kammen wrote, "Amerigo Vespucci became a source of international debate" over the origin of the name America. There were many
other theories of discoveries. "Christian abbots," for instance, "may
have reached the shores of North America eight hundred years before Columbus," and the "myth of a Welsh prince named Madoc, a
fabulous navigator, also enjoyed currency for a while."

Cristóbal Colón, Colombo, Colom, Colomb, or Christopher
Columbus, has "given his name to more geographical places than any
other actual figure in the history of the world, with the exception only
of Queen Victoria; in the United States he surpasses all other epo-
nyms except Washington," wrote Kirkpatrick Sale in *The Conquest
of Paradise*.

"Columbus sailed from Palos, Andalusia, on August third, with
three ships manned by a total company of about ninety, among whom
were at least six Jews," wrote Seymour Liebman in *The Jews in New
Spain*. Columbus had no monk or priest with him on the first voyage,
"in a time when no venture was undertaken without the presence of
a representative of the Church."

Kirkpatrick Sale argued that the evidence to support the historical
notion that Columbus was a Jew is circumstantial and "there is no

reason to give it credence." Simon Wiesenthal argues the opposite view in *The Secret Mission of Christopher Columbus.*

"Strangely, although he was 'world-famous' in his own day, Columbus, the itinerant traveler, has left us no record of his birth," wrote Newton Frohlich in an essay, "Was the Discoverer of America Jewish?" in *Moment.* "Many scholars agree with Spanish Christian historian Salvadore de Madariaga's assertion that Columbus was probably a *marrano,* a third-generation descendant of Jews who had converted to Christianity during Spain's antisemitic riots of 1391. The evidence—documents, diaries, letters, events that coincide—not only support de Madariaga's conclusion but also clarify who financed Columbus' voyage and why. But in Inquisition Spain, Columbus was forced to hide his Jewish origins."

Columbus, the *marrano* in search of an eternal haven, landed five centuries later in hundreds of historical studies. That a *marrano* would be celebrated as the discoverer of this nation, and, in the words of President Ronald Reagan, the "inventor of the American Dream," is an ironic weave of narrative histories; alas, the *marrano* must be an onerous signature to the antisemites.

Columbus has been invented in many faces and historical scenes over the past five hundred years; he has been created in numerous portraits, motivated in at least six new novels, captured for children in patriotic stories and miniature dioramas, and featured in sundries, national advertisements, and several commercial motion pictures.

Gerard Depardieu, for instance, is the most recent emergence of the adventurer in the new wave romance *1492: Conquest of Paradise,* directed by Ridley Scott. Columbus has never been worth more; not even the warrant of his tithe, at the time of his claim, would come close to the forty-five million dollars invested in the production of this quincentenary simulation.

"I was very happy to play Columbus, to give some idea of the man," said Depardieu in an interview in the *San Francisco Chronicle.* "Because who knows Columbus? Even historians know little about him. He was a Jew? We don't know. Spanish? Italian? Nothing is known about him."

"The most elaborate and fascinating attempt to prove that Columbus was a 'converso' Jew was made by Salvador de Madariaga in his vivid biography, *Christopher Columbus*, published in 1939," wrote John Noble Wilford in *The Mysterious History of Columbus*. "He contends that the family was Catalan Jewish. They first Latinized the surname 'Colón' into 'Columbus,' then adopted the Italian form of 'Columbo.' In Genoa, the family converted to Christianity," he noted. "Why did Las Casas write: 'In the matters of the Christian religion, no doubt, he was a Catholic and of much devotion'? Was there some doubt? Could his piety have been a diversionary tactic? Also, why the name changes? Other Genoese in Spain retained their Italian names, and besides, 'Colombo' is a perfectly good Spanish form. Madariaga concludes: 'May we point out how Jewish this all is? The men of the wandering race are so often bound to shift the conditions of their existence that, with them, change of name has become a habit, practically unknown though it is to the rest of mankind.' "

"If Jewish blood indeed ran in his veins, Columbus was wise to keep quiet about it, as he did concerning so much of his life before reaching Spain," observed Wilford. "But there is no proven substance to the Jewish hypothesis, and even less support for the related conjecture that his real purpose in undertaking the voyage was to find a homeland for Jews."

Stephen Greenblatt considered the "experience of the marvelous," the representation of tribal cultures in travel narratives and other documents that would have inspired the wonders and concepts of Columbus about the unknown and India. "In the late fifteenth century that concept depended principally on Marco Polo and Sir John Mandeville," he wrote in *Marvelous Possessions: The Wonder of the*

New World, "whose books Columbus read and quite possibly carried with him on his first voyage."

Columbus observed tribal people as savages, the simulations of his dominance; later, he would represent the absence of the tribes in his journal and written documents. The marvelous possessions in texts have no tribal or historical referent; the wonders of travel narratives are the manifest manners of dominance.

"Why did Columbus, who was carrying a passport and royal letters, think to take possession of anything, if he actually believed that he had reached the outlying regions of the Indies? It did not, after all, occur to Marco Polo in the late thirteenth century to claim for the Venetians any territorial rights in the East or to rename any of the countries; nor in the fourteenth century did Sir John Mandeville unfurl a banner on behalf of a European monarch," wrote Greenblatt. "The difference may be traced of course to the fact that, unlike Marco Polo or Mandeville, Columbus was neither a merchant nor a pilgrim: he was on a state-sponsored mission from a nation caught up in the enterprise of the *Reconquista*. But the objective of this mission has been notoriously difficult to determine." Tribal cultures could not dispute colonial claims because they were "not in the same universe of discourse."

Mandeville, the "knight of non-possession," was a marvelous liar, a fantastic anatomist, but his stories were no more burdensome to tribal survivance than colonialism, objectivism, and the literature of dominance. He mentioned the "Indians whose testicles hang down to the ground," and other textual envies. Greenblatt observed that "these marvels served as one of the principal signs of otherness and hence functioned not only as a source of fascination but of authentication."

Columbus was fortunate to have encountered the scholar Paolo dal Pozzo Toscanelli who had studied at the University of Florence and later at Padua. Paolo Emilio Taviani wrote in *Columbus: The Great Adventure* that "the fall of Constantinople to the Turk ruined many Venetian, Genoese, and Florentine families, particularly those involved in the spice trade. The Toscanelli family must have been preoccupied by these events and turned their gaze to the west to supplement the declining income from their commercial trade. There the land with the greatest promise was Portugal, not only because of its recent discoveries but also because it had before it an unknown and mysterious Ocean. If that mystery could be cleared up, science would be enriched. The world was growing smaller just when the need was being felt for wider space, new horizons."

Toscanelli, in a letter to Canon Fernando Martins of Lisbon, argued for the "shortest sea route from here to the Indies." That letter, dated 25 June 1474, was copied by Columbus five years later and is now at the Columbus Library in Seville. Toscanelli demonstrated with a globe that directly "opposite them to the west is shown the beginning of the Indies with the islands and places . . . bearing every kind of spice and gem and precious stone."

Columbus "kept a daily account of the voyage, the *Diario de a bordo*," or the *Onboard Log*. "Without doubt this was the most accurate and complete ship's log ever produced up to its time," wrote Fuson in *The Log of Christopher Columbus*. The original Log was presented to Queen Isabella. "With very little delay, she commanded a scribe to prepare an exact copy for the Admiral." This "version of the Log is known as the Barcelona copy."

Fuson points out that the "holograph original has not been seen since the death of Queen Isabella in 1504, and it is only presumed to have been in her possession up until that time." The Barcelona copy, with charts, manuscripts, and personal papers, was inherited by his eldest son, Diego, and then passed on to Luis, the grandson of Columbus. "The Barcelona copy of the *Diario de a bordo* was in Luis' possession in 1554, the year in which he was granted authorization to publish it. . . . He probably sold it to some member of the nobility who placed the manuscript in a private library, where it still lies hidden or whence it was destined eventually to disappear," but not before the manuscript "passed through the hands of Fray Bartolomé de las Casas, a Dominican friar and close personal friend of the Columbus family." Las Casas was eighteen years old in Seville when he witnessed the "triumphant return" of Columbus "from the first voyage." Carlos Sanz published a "truly innovative transcription" thirty years ago that "included a facsimile of the original document."

Columbus consulted the philosopher and theologian Pierre D'Ailly, "who discussed the earth's volume, the poles, climatic zones," wrote Jeffrey Burton Russell in *Inventing the Flat Earth*, and he "questioned the roundness of the earth only in the modern sense" that the sphere has mountains and is irregular. John Mandeville wrote marvelous travel narratives; he lied, but "his lies took place on a round earth."

Russell pointed out that the "untruth of the Flat Error lies in its incoherence as well as in its violation of facts. First there is the flat-out Flat Error that *never* before Columbus did anyone know that the world was round. This dismisses the careful calculations of the Greek geographers along with their medieval successors; it makes Aristotle, the most eloquent of round-earthers, and Ptolemy, the most accurate, into flat-earthers." Moreover, another "crude form of the Flat Error is the lurid embellishment that sailors feared that they would plunge off the edge of the flat earth if they voyaged too far out into the ocean."

Paolo Emilio Taviani observed that there are "no true portraits of Christopher Columbus. There are, however, over eighty statues or paintings, each quite different from the others because the artists were inspired by their own imagination, sometimes taking into account the few but essential descriptions about the physical appearance of the Genoese left to us by those who knew him." The simulations of the adventurer are based on four descriptions:

Don Ferdinand Columbus noted that his father was "well formed, taller than average with long face and rather high cheeks, neither fat nor skinny. He had an aquiline nose, light eyes, fair skin, and a healthy color. In his youth he had blond hair, but when he reached thirty it all turned white."

Bartolomé de las Casas saw Columbus at Santo Domingo at the turn of the century. "Concerning his person and outer appearance, he was tall, above average, his face long and authoritative, his nose aquiline, eyes blue, and complexion clear, tending to ruddy. His beard and hair were blond when he was young, but they turned white almost overnight from his travels."

Gonzalo Fernández de Oviedo wrote in *Historia general y natural de las Indias* that Columbus was a "man of good stature and fine appearance, taller than average and strong. His eyes were bright and his other features were well proportioned. His hair was very red, his visage reddish and freckled."

Taviani concluded that Angelo Trevisan, the personal secretary to the Venetian ambassador to Spain, observed that Columbus was a "tall man of distinguished bearing, reddish, with great intelligence and a long face."

Claudia Bushman noted in *America Discovers Columbus* that the "name Columbia was adopted as an alternative to America on the eve of the American Revolution." Phillis Wheatley, born a slave and later freed, was the first to use the name Columbia in her "poetic tribute to George Washington." She wrote, "One century scarce perform'd its destin'd round, When Gallic powers Columbia's fury found." Bushman wrote, "Columbia was the utopian land, newborn and full of promise." Philip Freneau and a "whole generation of poets, known as the 'rising glory school,' saw Columbia as the future hope of the world."

The 1893 Columbian Exposition in Chicago was a national broadside, a utopian theater of conservative inscriptions and eternal discoveries; events were scheduled everywhere to commemorate the four centuries and simulations of Columbus. "The Indian students from Carlisle, rennsylvania, marched in the school procession, where they were praised for smooth marching and regal carriage. A model Indian school thus demonstrated the 'civilization' of the natives," wrote Bushman. One repeated theme at that time was that "Columbus would never die but would live forever, honored and praised by each succeeding generation." The New World, however, "ignored him for the first two hundred years." The celebrations three centuries later were "decorous and dignified," and then, at last, the "business of the world halted to note his accomplishments" over the quadricentennial.

Kirkpatrick Sale pointed out that the "director of the American Republics, a division of the 1893 Columbian Exposition," wrote that the effigy of Christopher Columbus "had been 'painted and carved more often, perhaps than [that] of any other except the Savior of Mankind, and that the world is reminded of its obligation to him by more monuments than have been reared to the honor of any other hero of history.' "

Columbus pursued the marvelous other in the narratives of his time, searched for an eternal haven, landed in the simulations of mother earth, and was discovered, at last, in a constitutional democracy. Columbus is the long gaze of mother earth and the wonder of the nation. He was no trickster, no mediation of survivance, and his stories were denatured adventures, the translation of simulations into discoveries.

Mother, mother earth, the names so honored as tribal visions, could become the nonce words of civilization in the literature of dominance. That naive and sentimental nickname, a salutation to a common creation of nature, is the mere mother of manifest manners and the simulations of consumerism, reassured and tractable in the name of Christopher Columbus.

The best tribal stories were never rushed to their extinction in nature or reason. The wise hunters honored salamanders over the discoveries and simulations of mother earth, and endured the winter in the sure memories of their natural survivance. Not even the wicked shamans, or those predacious hunters in the fur trade, could chase the breath of nature out of their own stories. Starvation, disease, and soul death were worries of the heart, but honorable hunters were liberated in the shadows of their natural mediations, memories, visions, and stories. The radioactive ruins and chemical wastes of our time are new worries and without the narratives of regeneration. The winter memories of survivance are denied in the ruins of a chemical civilization.

The earth must bear, as no mother would, the abuses, banes, and miseries of manifest manners and discoveries. To name the wounded earth our mother, the insinuation of a wanton nurturance, is the avoidance of our own burdens in a nuclear nation.

Mother earth, the earth as our abused mother, is a misogynous metaphor traced to the long colonial gaze of Christopher Columbus. Once more, the narratives of our parents have been abandoned in the ruins of representations. We are the heirs, to be sure; at the same time, we are the orphans of our own dead tropes and narratives. We are the earth mutants, the lonesome survivors, who convene at night near the borders of tribal memories, creation, and treacherous observance.

"It is an indisputable fact that the concept of the earth goddess has grown strongest among the cultivating peoples," wrote Åke Hultkrantz in *The Religions of the American Indians*. "Many hunting tribes in North America manifest the same primitive belief in 'our mother,' 'mother earth.' The more recent peyote religion has accommodated Mother Earth to some extent under the influence of the Catholic cult of the Virgin Mary." The manifest notion of "primitive belief" is due no doubt to his patent on objective nature.

"Mother Earth will retaliate, the whole environment will retaliate, and the abusers will be eliminated," Russell Means maintained in *Mother Jones*. "Things will come full circle, back to where they started." He announced that "it is the role of American Indian peoples, the role of all natural beings, to survive." Means is a warrior of survivance.

Åke Hultkrantz and Russell Means seem to accede, with no sense of ironies, to the tribal creation notions of mother earth. Means avouches a natural order in the language of functional religion and resistance, a warrior bent to portraits and simulations. Hultkrantz inscribes the notion of mother earth as a universal representation of tribal favors and succors. He wrote in *Belief and Worship in Native North America* that "Mother Earth is a common idea among Indians over large parts of North America."

Sam Gill, however, wrote in *Mother Earth* that "the origins of Mother Earth as a Native American goddess were in some measure encouraged by the exigencies of the emergence of an 'Indian' identity that has complemented and often supplanted tribal identities." He pointed out that until "after the middle of this century, there is scant evidence that any Native American spoke of the earth as mother in any manner that could be understood as attesting to a major figure or a great goddess."

The stories of mother earth are the stories of a nation, and the nation discovered Christopher Columbus. How ironic then, that the discoveries of mother earth serve common tribal identities. Sam Gill argues that mother earth "may be recognized as being in continuity with a land ethos relatively common among Native American tribes, the conception of many elements of nature in personal, even kinship, terms." Mother earth "nurtures and gives identity to peoples who have lost their lands, yet who retain as central to their identity a respect and reverence for land and nature." Mother earth is a simulation, not a tribal reservation; mother is the absence of the real, the earth.

Laban Roborant, the salamander man, is a tribal trickster of the mundane. He is the reservation trace of the marvelous, and the solace of mother earth at a distance. His stories are aired to creation, natural reason, human unities, and the earth in the literature of survivance.

Roborant was born one lonesome winter on a woodland reservation; he studied philosophies, established his own school of amphibian meditation, and ruled a boat dock at the tribal marina.

He is the salamander of meditation in oral stories, the man of natural reason. The stories heard in nicknames are trickster hermeneutics. He would misuse the obvious to hear the best winter stories.

Roborant is a trickster healer who would overturn the sentiments of mother earth to embrace the traces of the moist snails on cold concrete. Early every morning he copies the snail trails at the marina and traces them on fish location maps for the tourists.

"We cast our hearts to the cold water, and the snails smear the same stories on the concrete overnight," he said on the boat dock. "Here we are at the end of the dock, domestic animals with an earth we named mother, and then we poison our natural relatives, and the memories of our own creation."

"The traces of tribal silence?"

"Survivance meditation," he said.

"Sounds like literary theory."

"Meditation is not theoretical," said Salamander.

"Snails were never my signature."

"Their traces end in our memories," he said. The salamander of the tribal marina menaced the black flies on the dock. He was more treacherous than nature, more elusive than winter bears, more obscure than spiders at the seams of civilization, more audacious than crows in the birch, even more memorable than the salamanders in his meditation. Salamander was the natural reason and ironies of the earth in his own stories.

Mother Earth is the nickname of a tribal man who once lived in a paradise of black flies on a woodland reservation. The lake near his cabin was decorated with rich ribbons of natural light that summer. The rush of dawn touched the stones on the natural shore at the tribal marina and landed later in weakened shadows behind the medicine poles. Hundreds of black flies waited on the boat dock for the first glance of the sunrise, the sudden beams that would warm their wings into motion and flight.

"Black flies remember our creation," said Mother Earth.

"Not on this dock," said Salamander. He beat the sun to bash the black flies on the rails of the wooden dock, and then he brushed their remains into the water. The bodies of the flies floated near shore without honor, even the fish seemed to wait for the wings to move as a lure. The sun bounced on the water and roused the bodies of the wounded flies; their wings buzzed and turned in wild circles.

"There, listen to the flies, the signatures of creation even at their death," said Mother Earth. He leaned over the water and handed the cold bodies to the warm stones. The flies buzzed in the sun.

"Flies are bait not stories," said Salamander.

"Black flies are the earth mothers," said Mother Earth.

"No mothers here," said Salamander.

"Black flies are my relatives," said Mother Earth.

"Must be your cousins," said Salamander. He crushed more flies on the dock with his wide hand. "There, more relatives to mourn over on the stones." He raised three flies to the sun and then pulled out their wings.

"Black flies are my stories," said Mother Earth.

"Now you tell me," said Salamander.

"Thousands of black flies live on my name."

"You must mean live on your body," said Salamander. He covered his nose with his hands. Mother Earth never washed and he wore the same stained shirt for more than a year. The fetor of Mother Earth has raised hundreds of generations of grateful black flies. When he moved into the light the flies circled his head and crotch in great black orbits.

"They land on my middle name."

"Do the flies have nicknames?"

"More than one," said Mother Earth.

"Then you are the man of this house of mother flies?"

"You boast, but the earth hears the flies."

"Mother, my stories are about salamanders."

"Black flies are the same."

"Wash your body once and your relatives are gone."

"Once, many years ago, there were four flies caught in a bottle right on my desk," said Mother Earth. "We heard them buzz and watched them weaken day after day, and near the end, one after the other, they marched in circles close to the rim and then died upside down."

"Mother, are you ready to fly?"

"Almost every morning, summer and winter, for months and months after their death, the wings of the flies would buzz when the first blaze of sunlight bounced in the bottle," said Mother Earth.

"Weird suckers," said Salamander.

"Those black flies were the sound of creation."

"What kind of bottle was it?"

"Something in clear glass," said Mother Earth.

"Black flies sound much better in aluminum."

"To the ordinary person, the body of humanity seems vast," wrote Brian Walker in *Hua Hu Ching*, the teachings of Lao Tzu. "In truth, it is neither bigger nor smaller than anything else. To the ordinary person, there are others whose awareness needs raising. In truth, there is no self, and no other. To the ordinary person, the temple is sacred and the field is not. This, too, is a dualism which runs counter to the truth."

Mother Earth liberates black flies in the literature of survivance. The earth has been wounded with discoveries. The rivers, birds, animals, and insects have been poisoned near the universities. Salamander crushes black flies, and we are the pronouns of meditation in his name, we are the touch and remembrance of the salamander earth. We bear the wounds and the literature of the earth. Must the discoveries and remembrance of the earth be an obscure suicide?

Salamander hears the water rise with the sun over the tribal marina. You are the salamander earth, and you must remember the literature of our survivance. Silence is human, not natural. Salamander crushes the slow black flies, never to extinction, but *you* are his closure in stories. Mother Earth rescues and liberates his relatives, the black flies of natural reason, every morning from the cold water.

5

ISHI OBSCURA

Ishi was never his real name.

Ishi is a simulation, the absence of his tribal names. He posed at the borders of the camera, the circles of photographers and spectators, in the best backlighted pictures of the time.

Ishi was never his real name, and he is not the photographs of that tribal man captured three generations ago in a slaughterhouse in northern California. He was thin and wore a canvas shirt then, a man of natural reason, a lonesome hunter, but never the stout postiche of a wild man lost and found in a museum. Two tribal men were captured, two pronouns in a museum, one obscure and the other endured in silence. Ishi the obscura is discovered with a bare chest in photographs; the tribal man named in that simulation stared over the camera, into the distance.

Ishi is not the last man of stone. He is not the obscure other, the mortal silence of savagism and the vanishing race. The other pronoun is not the last crude measure of uncivilization; the silence of that tribal man is not the dead voice of racial photographs and the vanishing pose. He came out of the mountains in an undershirt; later, he was redressed in Western clothes in the museum, and then he was told to bare his chest for the curious writers and photographers.

Ishi told stories to be heard, not recorded and written; he told stories to be heard as the sounds of remembrance, and with a sense of time that would never be released in the mannered silence of a museum. Overnight he became the last of the stone, the everlasting unknown, the man who would never vanish in the cruel ironies of civilization.

Ishi was given a watch "which he wore and kept wound but not set," wrote Theodora Kroeber in *Ishi in Two Worlds*. He understood time by the sun and other means, but his "watch was an article of pride and beauty to be worn with chain and pendant, not a thing of utility."

This tribal survivor evaded the barbarians in the mountains, the summer tourists, and the unnatural miners in search of precious minerals; now, as a captured portrait, he endures the remembrance of their romantic heirs. The gaze of those behind the camera haunts the unseen margins of time and scene in the photograph; the obscure presence of witnesses at the simulation of savagism could become the last epiphanies of a chemical civilization.

He was invited to return to the mountains and asked by his admirers to start a fire in the natural way; he was reluctant at first, but then he showed his reentry students, an anthropologist and a distinguished medical doctor, how to hunt with various bows and arrows. He heard the rush of mountain water, the wind over stone, and he told stories the bears were sure to hear, but he could have told his students even more about the violence of civilization. The miners were the real savages; they had no written language, no books, no manners of providence, no sense of humor, no natural touch, no museums, no stories in the blood, and their harsh breath, even at a great distance, poisoned the seasons. They were the agents of civilization.

Ishi came out of the mountains and was invited to a cultural striptease at the centerfold of manifest manners and the histories of dominance; he crossed the scratch line of savagism and civilization with one name, and outlived the photographers. His survivance, that sense of mediation in tribal stories, is heard in a word that means "one of the people," and that word became his name. So much the better, and he never told the anthropologists, reporters, and curious practitioners his sacred tribal name, not even his nicknames. The other tribal pronoun endured in silence. He might have said, "The ghosts were generous in the silence of the museum, and now these men pretend to know me in their name." Trickster hermeneutics is the silence of his nicknames.

"Ishi is the absence," he might have said.

"He was the last of his tribe," wrote Mary Ashe Miller in the *San Francisco Call*, September 6, 1911. He "feared people" and "wandered, alone, like a hunted animal. . . . The man is as aboriginal in his mode of life as though he inhabited the heart of an African jungle, all of his methods are those of primitive peoples."

Ishi became the absence of his stories of survivance, the wild other to those he trusted in silence. There were other names in the mountains. The notion of the aboriginal and the primitive combined both racialism and postmodern speciesism, a linear consideration that was based on the absence of monotheism, material evidence of civilization, institutional violence, and written words more than on the presence of imagination, oral stories, the humor in trickster stories, and the observation of actual behavior and experience.

Miller wrote that hunting "has been his only means of living and that has been done with bow and arrow of his own manufacture, and with snares. Probably no more interesting individual could be found today than this nameless Indian." Indeed, the simulation and pronoun of absence in the stories of survivance.

Ishi smiled, shrugged his shoulders, and looked past the camera, over the borders of covetous civilization, into the distance. The witnesses and nervous photographers, he might have wondered, were lost and lonesome in their own technical activities. Whatever they valued in the creation of the other they had lost in the causal narratives of their own lives.

Susan Sontag wrote in *On Photography* that photographs are "experience captured, and the camera is the ideal arm of consciousness in its acquisitive mood." The camera captures others, not the experiences of the photographer; the presence of the other is discovered in a single shot, the material reduction of a pose, the vanishing pose, and then invented once more in a collection of pictures. The simulation of a tribe in photographs.

The tribes have become the better others, to be sure, and the closer the captured experiences are to the last wild instances in the world, the more valuable are the photographs. Nothing, of course, was ever last that can be seen in a picture. Nothing is last that are stories of remembrance; nothing is last because the last is the absence of stories.

The camera creates an instance that never existed in tribal stories; the last and lost was not in tribal poses but in the remembrance of the witnesses who died at the borders of their possessions behind the camera. To be heard was once a course of survivance in tribal imagination; now, however, the tribes must prove with photographs the right to be seen and heard as the other. Mere presence is never the last word at the borders and margins of civilization; the sounds of stories, the human touch of humor and silence, and visions must be documented with photographs. Simulations are the outset and bear our tribal presence at the borders.

Sontag argues that "there is something predatory in the act of taking a picture. To photograph people is to violate them, by seeing them as they never see themselves, by having knowledge of them they can never have; it turns people into objects that can be symbolically possessed."

The absence of the tribes is sealed, not real, in a photograph; the absence is a simulation, the causal narratives of museum consciousness, and the remorse of civilization. Photographs are the discoveries of the absence of the tribes. Tribal stories, on the other hand, are mediations, and more is heard, seen, and remembered in oral stories than in a thousand pictures.

"The primitive notion of the efficacy of images presumes that images possess the qualities of real things," wrote Sontag, "but our inclination is to attribute to real things the qualities of an image." The simulation supersedes the real and remembrance.

Ishi told an interpreter, "I will live like the white people from now on." The Bureau of Indian Affairs had promised him protection, but he would remain with his friends in the museum. The ironies of "protection" have weakened the language of government. Ishi would not hear the promise of the miner, but he had no reason at the time to be suspicious of an agency created to represent his interests. "I want to stay where I am, I will grow old here, and die in this house." Tuberculosis ended his life five years later.

Alfred Kroeber, the anthropologist who cared for Ishi, wrote that "he never swerved from his first declaration." He lived and worked in the museum. "His one great dread, which he overcame but slowly, was of crowds." Ishi said, "hansi saltu," when he saw the ocean and the crowded beach for the first time. The words were translated as "many white people."

Kroeber, an eminent academic humanist, is seldom remembered for his nicknames. Ishi, on the other hand, remembered the anthropologist as his "big chiep," which was his common pronunciation of the word "chief." Ishi used the tribal word "saltu," or "white man," a word that could be used as a nominal nickname commensurate with his own—Big Chiep Kroeber, the anthropologist, and Ishi, the mountain man who told survivance stories.

Ishi was captured and possessed forever by the camera, not the agencies of a wild government. The sheriff secured "a pathetic figure crouched upon the floor," the *Oroville Register* reported on August 29, 1911. "The canvas from which his outer shirt was made had been roughly sewed together. His undershirt had evidently been stolen in a raid upon some cabin. His feet were almost as wide as they were long, showing plainly that he had never worn either moccasins or shoes. In his ears were rings made of buckskin thongs."

Sheriff Webber "removed the cartridges from his revolver" and ."gave the weapon to the Indian. The aborigine showed no evidence that he knew anything regarding its use. A cigarette was offered to him, and while it was very evident that he knew what tobacco was, he had never smoked it in that form, and had to be taught the art."

Alfred Kroeber confirmed the newspaper report and contacted the sheriff who "had put the Indian in jail not knowing what else to do with him since no one around town could understand his speech or he theirs," wrote Theodora Kroeber in *Alfred Kroeber: A Personal Configuration*. "Within a few days the Department of Indian Affairs authorized the sheriff to release the wild man to the custody of Kroeber and the museum staff. . . ." Ishi was housed in rooms furnished by Phoebe Apperson Hearst. She had created the Department and Museum of Anthropology at the University of California.

Kroeber pointed out that "he has perceptive powers far keener than those of highly educated white men. He reasons well, grasps an idea quickly, has a keen sense of humor, is gentle, thoughtful, and courteous and has a higher type of mentality than most Indians."

Thomas Waterman, the linguist at the museum, administered various psychological tests at the time and concluded in a newspaper interview that "this wild man has a better head on him than a good many college men."

These college men, however, were the same men who discovered and then invented an outsider, the last of his tribe, with their considerable influence and power of communication. They were not insensitive, to be sure, but their studies and museums would contribute to the simulations of savagism. At the same time, some of these educated men were liberal nihilists, and their academic strategies dispraised civilization. These men who represented civilization would find in the other what they had not been able to find in themselves or their institutions; the simulations of the other became the antiselves of their melancholy.

"The bourgeois literary scholar who strikes a pose and stigmatizes boredom as a cross the aristocracy has to bear forgets that it was boredom that engendered literature," wrote Wolf Lepenies in *Melancholy and Society*. "Bourgeois melancholy signifies a form of loss of world which is considerably different from that entailed in aristocratic melancholy. The latter resulted from a loss of world, the former from having relinquished a world that had never been possessed."

Ishi trusted his new world, and those who honored him were bettered in their careers. He had been liberated from violence and starvation in the mountains; a wild transformation from the silhouette of the hunted to the heuristic pleasures of a museum.

Kroeber wrote that he "put on weight rapidly after coming within reach of the fleshpots of civilization and their three times a day recurrence. In a couple of months he had gained between forty and fifty pounds."

At the University of California a week later, "the unknown refused to obey orders" for the first time. "He was to be photographed in a garment of skins, and when the dressing for the aboriginal part began he refused to remove his overalls," reported Mary Ashe Miller in the *San Francisco Call*. "He say he not see any other people go without them," said the tribal translator Sam Batwi, "and he say he never take them off no more."

Miller wrote that the "battery of half a dozen cameras focused upon him was a new experience and evidently a somewhat terrifying one. He stood with his head back and a half smile on his face, but his compressed lips and dilated nostrils showed that he was far from happy. . . . His name, if he knows it, he keeps to himself. It is considered bad form among aboriginal tribes, I am told, to ask any one's name, and it is seldom divulged until a firm basis of friendship is established."

Theodora Kroeber wrote that "Ishi was photographed so frequently and so variously that he became expert on matters of lighting, posing, and exposure. . . . Photographs of him were bought or made to be treasured as mementos along with family pictures and camera records of a holiday or an excursion."

You hear his name now in the isolation of his photographs. You must imagine the lonesome humor in the poses that pleased the curators in the natural light near the museum at the University of California. Their dead voices haunt the margins of our photographs. You were not the last to dream in his stories. You were not the last memories of the tribes, but you were the last to land in a museum as the simulations of a vanishing pose in photographs.

Ishi may have undressed above the waist to pose for the photograph supervised by Joseph Kossuth Dixon, or one of his assistants, in connection with an incredible enterprise to capture the last images of a vanishing race: the Rodman Wanamaker Expedition of Citizenship to the North American Indian in 1913.

Dixon outfitted a private railroad car and traveled to many tribal communities and museums around the country. Later that year he published a portrait of Ishi and more than a hundred other photographs from his collection in *The Vanishing Race*.

"The Wanamaker expeditions took place at a time when the sense of national guilt about what had been done to the Indians was rising," wrote Charles Reynolds, Jr. in *American Indian Portraits from the Wanamaker Expedition of 1913*. "The Indians were seen as noble savages whom the white man had turned into a vanishing race." Ishi and Bluff Creek Tom are the only two "noble savages" who are not dressed to the neck in the collection of photographs.

Ishi posed for this "given" photograph, one of the few with his chest bared. The apparent tattoo on his chest does not appear in any other photographs of him published in *Ishi in Two Worlds* by Theodora Kroeber. The tattoo, an intentional retouch or accidental stain on the negative, has never been explained. The simulated tattoo, or negative stain, enhances the image of a naked savage.

Saxton Pope, the surgeon at the medical school near the museum, was a student of tribal archery and other tribal activities. He took Ishi to Buffalo Bill's Wild West Show when it was in the city. "He always enjoyed the circus, horseback feats, clowns, and similar performances," he wrote in "The Medical History of Ishi." Later, a "warrior bedecked in all his paint and feathers, approached us. The two Indians looked at each other in absolute silence for several minutes. The Sioux then spoke in perfect English, saying: 'What tribe of Indian is this?' I answered, 'Yana, from Northern California.'

"The Sioux then gently picked up a bit of Ishi's hair, rolled it between his fingers, looked critically into his face, and said, 'He is a very high grade of Indian.' As we left, I asked Ishi what he thought of the Sioux. Ishi said, 'Him's big chiep. . . .' "

Ishi was a winsome warrior of survivance, not a religious leader or a warrior chief on the road to complement the tragic simulations and representations of tribal cultures. His personal power was more elusive than the political poses of a tribal leader. He was never obligated to speak as a leader or the last hunter of his tribe; otherwise, his stories might not have been heard, not even in the museum. His stories were his survivance, and not an obligation to be a tribal leader. He had a natural smile, but he never learned how to shake hands.

Pierre Clastres wrote in *Society Against the State* that a tribal chief must "prove his command over words. Speech is an imperative obligation for the chief." The leader "must submit to the obligation to speak, the people he addresses, on the other hand, are obligated only to appear not to hear him."

Some tribal leaders were captured as proud warriors in photographs; they were heard, overhead as simulations too much, and translated without reason, and out of season; their stories were lost to manifest manners, and lost at inaugurations and postmodern performances in wild west shows. The simulated leaders lost their eminence in the discourse of tribal power, "because the society itself, and not the chief, is the real locus of power."

Clastres overturns the rustic notions of tribal leaders with a new sense of political responsibilities in communities. "The chief's obligations to speak, that steady flow of empty speech that he *owes* the tribe, is his infinite debt, the guarantee that prevents the man of speech from becoming a man of power."

Ishi was never heard as a tribal leader. He bared his chest and posed for photographs, but he was never decorated as a warrior. His portrait was published with a collection of other simulated tribal people. He posed for friends and photographers, but he was never invited to bare his chest at a wild west show.

"En route to the inauguration of President Wilson in 1913, thirty-two chiefs stopped in Philadelphia for the day to be entertained at the Wanamaker Store," wrote John Wanamaker in *American Indian Portraits*. The special luncheon of warriors was followed by a "war dance" in a private corporate office.

Ishi lived and worked in a museum. He never wore leather clothes or feathers, and he was not invited to pose at the presidential inauguration. He was not a chief, but as a tribal survivor he could have been seen and heard as a leader. In a sense, he had more power than those who were invited to the inauguration as decorated warriors. Tribal power is more communal than personal, and the power of the spoken word goes with the stories of the survivors, and becomes the literature of survivance.

Ishi was at "ease with his friends," wrote Theodora Kroeber. He "loved to joke, to be teased amiably and to tease in return. And he loved to talk. In telling a story, if it were long or involved or of considerable affect, he would perspire with the effort, his voice rising toward a falsetto of excitement." His stories must have come from visual memories, and he should be honored for more than his stories, his humor, and survivance: he should be honored because he never learned how to slow his stories down to be written and recorded.

"The Rodman Wanamaker Expedition of Citizenship to the North American Indian concluded in December 1913 with a ceremony on the Staten Island site where ground had been broken for the Indian memorial ten months earlier," wrote Charles Fergus in *Shadow Catcher*, a novel based on the unusual photographic expedition.

"At the Panama-Pacific Exposition of 1915, in San Francisco, former president Theodore Roosevelt opened the exhibit of expeditionary photographs, and Joseph Dixon lectured three times a day for five months to more than a million citizens. Prints were sold from the three Wanamaker expeditions, perhaps the first photographic print sales on record," wrote Fergus in the epilogue. "Dixon's illustrated book, *The Vanishing Race*, was also selling briskly; it has been reprinted several times over the years, with critics favorably comparing his photographs to the famous Indian portraits of Edward S. Curtis."

The Wanamaker photographs were forgotten in a few years' time; the collection landed in an attic and later in museums and archives. Those behind the cameras have vanished, but the last wild man and other tribal people captured in photographs have been resurrected in a nation eager to create a tragic history of the past.

The Indian agent James McLaughlin, wrote Fergus, "was instrumental in persuading Franklin Lane, Secretary of the Interior under President Wilson, to speed the granting of citizenship to qualified Indians." The tribes were discovered, captured, removed to reservations, and photographed as outsiders in their own land. Ishi died eight years before he might have become a citizen of the mountains he remembered and told in many, many stories. "McLaughlin designed tokens of citizenship that were presented in 1916 and 1917. These consisted of a purse . . . a leather bag, a button."

Ishi and then his photograph ended in a museum. The photographers were lost on the margins; those who gazed at his bare chest and waited to shake his hand would vanish three generations later in a lonesome and melancholy civilization.

Ishi has become one of the most discoverable tribal names in the world; even so, he has seldom been heard as a real person. Ishi "looked upon us as sophisticated children," wrote Saxton Pope. "We knew many things, and much that is false. He knew nature, which is always true," and his "soul was that of a child, his mind that of a philosopher."

Theodora Kroeber wrote that "Ishi was living for the summer with the Waterman family where Edward Sapir, the linguist, would be coming in a few weeks to work with him, recording Ishi's Yahi dialect of the Yana language. . . . They noticed that he was eating very little and appeared listless and tired. Interrupting the work with Sapir, they brought Ishi to the hospital where Pope found what he and Kroeber had most dreaded, a rampant tuberculosis."

Ishi died at noon on March 25, 1916. Kroeber was in New York at the time and wrote in a letter, "As to disposal of the body, I must ask you as my personal representative to yield nothing at all under any circumstances. If there is any talk about the interests of science, say for me that science can go to hell. We propose to stand by our friends. . . . We have hundreds of Indian skeletons that nobody ever comes near to study. The prime interest in this case would be of a morbid romantic nature."

Four days later the *San Mateo Labor Index* reported that "the body of Ishi, last of the Yana tribe of Indians, was cremated Monday at Mount Olivet cemetery. It was according to the custom of his tribe and there was no ceremony." Saxton Pope created a death mask, "a very beautiful one." The pottery jar that held the ashes of Ishi was placed in a rock cairn.

6

CASINO COUPS

Luther Standing Bear must have wondered about a civilization that would count coup with coins. He seemed to envision, on his way to a government school with other children, the contradictions that would ensue in the creation of casinos, and the contention over tribal sovereignty on reservations.

The Lakota activist and author was raised a century ago to be a hunter and warrior, but the federal government had terminated the buffalo and then removed tribal families to reservations. He was one of the first children to be educated at the government school in Carlisle, Pennsylvania.

"I was thinking of my father," he wrote in *My People the Sioux*, "and how he had many times said to me, 'Son, be brave! Die on the battlefield if necessary away from home. It is better to die young than to get old and sick and then die.' When I thought of my father, and how he had smoked the pipe of peace, and was not fighting any more, it occurred to me that this chance to go East would prove that I was brave if I were to accept it."

Standing Bear wrote that when "the train stopped" in Sioux City "we raised the windows to look out." The "white people were yelling at us and making a great noise," and they "started to throw money at us. We little fellows began to gather up the money, but the larger boys told us not to take it, but to throw it back at them. They told us if we took the money the white people would put our names in a big book. We did not have sense enough then to understand that those white people had no way of discovering what our names were. However, we threw the money all back at them. At this, the white people laughed and threw more money at us."

Five generations later many of the tribes that endured colonial cruelties, the miseries of hunger, disease, coercive assimilation, and manifest manners are now moneyed casino patrons and impresarios on reservations.

The white people are throwing money at the tribes once more, but not to tribal children at train stations; millions of dollars are lost each month at bingo, blackjack, electronic slot machines, and other mundane games of chance at casinos located on reservation land. The riches, for some, are the new wampum, or the curious coup count of lost coins. The weird contradiction is that the enemies of tribalism have now become the sources of conditional salvation; this could be the converse of an eternal tribal millennial movement that was last heard in the Ghost Dance.

This preposterous carnival of coup coins has transformed tribal communities. The reservation governments throw nothing back to the states in fees or taxation, and that is one of the serious concerns of tribal sovereignty.

More than a hundred tribes are reported to have casinos or gaming facilities on and near reservations in the nation; the losses by the patrons at these operations, estimated to be several billion dollars a year, have become the extreme sources of tribal revenue. The ironies of panindian casino reparations could become the wages of sovereignty.

The Indian Gaming Regulatory Act, passed in 1988, recognized that the tribes have the "exclusive right to regulate gaming" if the activity is not prohibited by federal or state laws. The new gaming regulations established a National Indian Gaming Commission to meet congressional concerns and to "protect such gaming as a means of generating tribal revenue."

The new law established three classes of gaming: the first, traditional tribal games; the second, games such as bingo, lotto, and pulltabs; the third, and the most controversial of the classes, includes lotteries, slot machines, blackjack, pari-mutuel betting, and other casino type games. The tribes with the third class of casino games are required to negotiate with the state to enter into a "compact governing the conduct of gaming activities."

In the past few years there have been more news stories about tribal casinos than any other tribal activities. The *New York Times* has published numerous reports on the enormous Foxwoods Casino, owned and operated by the Mashantucket Pequot Indians. Governor Lowell Weicker of Connecticut reached an agreement with the new casino to permit slot machines, required, in part, by the new federal gaming laws. The envies are unnatural when a tribal casino has the riches to negotiate with the governor; this agreement weakens possible legislation that would allow other casinos to operate as a source of much needed revenue in the state. The Pequot Indians agreed to contribute at least a million dollars a year "in gambling profits to a fund to aid troubled cities and towns."

The governor has resisted casinos in the state, including those located on reservations, "on moral and economic grounds," reported The *New York Times*. His agreement with the tribe was a concession that resisted an "even greater evil; the building of casinos throughout the state." The Mirage Resorts of Las Vegas had "offered to build a casino in Hartford or Bridgeport."

Minnesota has negotiated agreements with thirteen casinos on eleven reservations in the state. The *Minneapolis Star Tribune* reported that tribal gaming employed more people in the state than United Parcel Service or Burlington Northern Railroad. "Lump the six casinos together, and they are the 20th largest employer in Minnesota," with about five thousand employees." The Mystic Lake Casino, owned by the Shakopee Mdewakanton Sioux, seats more than a thousand people at bingo and operates at least as many slot machines. The Shooting Star Casino on the White Earth Reservation cost more than sixteen million dollars to build, and the tribe has plans to build an addition that would double the size of the casino.

Many tribes "contracted with private gambling firms to set up and manage their gaming operations," reported Iri Carter for The Center for Urban and Regional Affairs at the University of Minnesota. "Several of these firms took the lion's share of the profits and left outstanding debts. Tribes had no choice but to ask for federal assistance."

The National Indian Gaming Commission was established to review contracts and to protect "gaming as a means of generating tribal revenue." The Inspector General for the Department of the Interior reported last year that management companies and some contractors had diverted millions of dollars from tribal casinos. "There may be some ticking time bombs" out there, said the inspector, James Richards.

Chris Ison reported in the *Minneapolis Star Tribune* that "the manager at Fortune Bay Casino" in northern Minnesota was replaced "after some tribal members alleged a conflict of interest. The manager, Cyril Kauchick, and an attorney for the casino, Kent Tupper, held an interest in the company that leased slot machines to the casino." Later, casino representatives said that "the federal report criticizing Indian gambling operations was 'political sabotage' intended to feed public mistrust of the industry." The Minnesota Indian Gaming Association "called the report inaccurate, paternalistic and part of a broad campaign by Las Vegas interests and others to 'weaken tribal gaming and undermine the sovereignty of tribal governments.'" Those named in the report denied that their interests and profits were improper. Tupper said he "had disclosed his ownership interests in Creative Games and stepped down as tribal attorney at the end of 1991."

The Bureau of Indian Affairs reported in *Indian News* that last year twenty tribes in two states, Michigan and Minnesota, provided close to eight thousand jobs with an annual payroll of more than ninety million dollars. The report indicated that the casinos generate more than eleven million dollars in annual social security and medicare tax revenue, more than two million dollars in state and federal unemployment compensation, and the casinos have reduced the cost of welfare in the two states. The new riches of the tribes translate as political power, and that in a slow and envious economy.

The number of casinos and employees grows by the month, and the estimated several billion dollars in the losses of patrons has increased at a rate that could save several state budgets from ruin.

Anishinaabe singers are the heirs of a rich tradition of chance and games, the moccasin games. Four objects are covered with two pairs of moccasins; one object is marked and becomes the chance of the game. None of this is done without music and the beat of a drum. The songs have no words; some of the best music of the tribe was inspired by the chance of the moccasin games. The best moccasin game songs were heard in dreams and visions, and the song, with the beat of the drum, accented beats and then hesitation, enchances the game, and teases the players to choose the moccasins that covered the unmarked object.

There are no traditional songs to tease the electronic machines; the coins are the sounds of technology, the possession of time and place without music. The tease of chance is in the casino stories not the songs. The chance has no association of communities, no dreams of the hidden objects, and the winners lose their stories at the tribal casinos.

Standing Bear was naive on that train to a government school, but later he wrote several books and weathered the contradictions of his time. His name was entered in the "big book" for other reasons, but he, and other tribal leaders, might have warned the impresarios of the tribes that the riches of casinos entice the envies of others and could be the ruin of tribal sovereignty.

The casinos have raised new contradictions, the bereavement of traditional tribal values, and the envies of outsiders. The more money that is lost at casino games, the greater the revenues, and because of the riches, the elections of tribal leaders become more extreme on reservations.

The Mohawks at Akwesasne, for instance, came to violence over the casinos located on their reserve. One side fought for casinos and sovereignty, and the other side, the elected tribal leaders, opposed gambling operations in their communities. Two tribal people were killed and a casino was damaged before the onslaught ended several years ago.

"The allure of fast tax-free money inflamed and emboldened the Mohawks who entered the gambling business, even as it weakened those holding on to the old ways," wrote Rick Hornung in *One Nation Under the Gun: Inside the Mohawk Civil War.* "A new class of bingo chiefs were beating the odds, dealing with the white economy on favorable terms. The traditionalists counterattacked, claiming that Mohawk life was being corrupted by men who profit from games of chance rather than work. White bureaucrats and politicians, police and prosecutors initially saw this dispute as a brawl over gambling." The Mohawks, however, saw this as a threat to their traditional way of life.

The Red Lake Band of Chippewa Indians in Minnesota and the Mescalero Apache Tribe of New Mexico have sued agencies of the federal government to declare the new gaming laws unconstitutional and to prohibit the appointment of the National Indian Gaming Commission. The essential issue is tribal sovereignty.

The claim of the tribes is that the Indian Gaming Regulatory Act "violates their sovereign prerogatives to conduct affairs on their lands as permitted by treaties and the Indian Self Determination Act," wrote William Thompson in *Indian Gaming and the Law*. "They especially object to the fact that the Act determined the legality of their gaming enterprise on the basis of state law." To conduct casino games, the third class of gaming, the tribes must "make agreements with state governments. Their claim is that their standing is a matter of federal and not state law, and that any matters governing their commercial activities must be established through federal, not state law."

Most tribes have either avoided or disputed the regulation that the third class of games, those that have raised the most revenue at casinos, must be negotiated with state governments. Tribal leaders maintain that casinos are located on sovereign tribal land, outside of state jurisdiction. Nonetheless, federal agents raided casinos and seized machines to enforce the gaming laws on five reservations in Arizona. The seizure was blocked by angry tribal people on one reservation until the governor agreed to negotiate the issue.

At the "Fort McDowell Yavapai Reservation, outside nearby Scottsdale," reported The *New York Times*, "a group of about 100 Indians used three dozen or so pickups, big earth-movers and other vehicles to surround eight trucks that were preparing to carry game machines away from the parking lot of the casino there.

"The blockade by the Indians, none of whom appeared to be carrying weapons, trapped not only the trucks but also dozens of F.B.I. agents. The ensuing standoff lasted five hours and was not broken until" the governor agreed to negotiate.

Tim Giago, editor of *The Lakota Times*, said, "There is a lot of anger in Indian country over this. The Indian nations are sick and tired of being treated like children. These are sovereign lands. Why in hell should these lands need the state's permission?"

Governor Fife Symington was concerned about violence over casinos on tribal land. "We could be headed for a real crisis and showdown," he told a reporter for The *New York Times*. "This is just the fuse that leads to a larger keg of dynamite. Let's face facts: What we're dealing with here is the terribly emotional issue of sovereignty on these lands." The governor negotiated a seven-year compact with the tribe and the video poker machines were returned to the casino.

Governor Symington, however, signed a new statute several months later that prohibits casino gambling within the borders of Arizona. "The measure, which outlaws even casino nights sponsored by churches and small charities to raise money," reported The *New York Times*, "is the latest example of a backlash in a number of states against" the third class of casino games on reservations. Some tribal leaders indicated that "they would begin a petition drive seeking a referendum to have the measure overturned." The new law has brought some churches and casino reservations together in a common cause. "John Lewis, head of the Arizona Intertribal Council, said the petition drive would be backed by a 'broad coalition' of Indians and charitable organizations."

Nelson Rose, a law professor, wrote in *Indian Gaming and the Law* that one part of the new criminal statutes "revolutionizes Indian and criminal law by making it a federal crime to violate any state law involving gambling on Indian land." He concludes, however, that "the reality will probably be no enforcement at all, since even the federal government has limited resources and gambling crimes are the lowest priority offenses."

William Thompson argued that the essential "control over Indian gaming should be national." The issues of tribal sovereignty "are difficult and they are clearly controversial. What is clear, though, is that the vast majority of tribes do not want any state regulation whatsoever. They should not be required to come under state regulations."

Tribal sovereignty is inherent, an essential right that has been *limited* but not *given* by the government. Congress, however, negotiated the original treaties with the tribes and has the absolute power to terminate reservations. That tension, between the idea of limited sovereignty and assimilation, could be resolved in federal courts or by congressional resolutions in favor of state governments. Casinos could be the last representation of tribal sovereignty. The winners hear the envies and could become the losers.

Tribal sovereignty is inherent, and that sense of independence and territorial power has been the defense of sovereignty on tribal land and reservations. Federal courts and congressional legislation have limited the absolute practices of sovereignty, such as certain criminal and civil responsibilities on reservations, but that sense of inherent sovereignty prevails in the many interpretations of the treaties with the federal government. The Indian Gaming Regulatory Act has placed tribal sovereignty in competition with the sovereignty of the states. Sovereignty is not, however, a limited issue or idea in the histories of other states and nations.

"The concept of sovereignty originated in the closer association of the developing state and the developing community which became inevitable when it was discovered that power had to be shared between them," wrote F. H. Hinsley in *Sovereignty*. "The function of the concept was to provide the only formula which could ensure the effective exercise of power once this division of power or collaboration of forces had become inescapable."

The Coalition to Protect Community and States' Rights has been active in the defense of state sovereignty. The stated mission of the Coalition is to "seek clarification of the federal Indian gaming law so as to restore a level playing field between Indian gambling and other forms of legalized gambling, and to protect communities and states which oppose it from having unwanted and untaxed gambling thrust upon them." There is nothing in their stated mission, objectives, or proposed action that mentions treaties or the inherent sovereignty of the tribes.

The envies of casino riches incite the enemies of the tribes and those who oppose the sovereignty honored for more than a century in treaties with the federal government. The envies, of course, are the manifest manners of domination, the oppression, and miseries of racialism. Tribal sovereignty, in this sense, could be weakened only if the casino tribes were enervated by their own new wealth, and were seen as being powerless.

"Only wealth without power or aloofness without policy are felt to be parasitical, useless, revolting, because such conditions cut" the associations of people, argued Hannah Arendt in *Antisemitism*. The envies of others, those who would hate the tribes for their wealth without power, are terrible burdens of tribal sovereignty.

Standing Bear heard the last of the Ghost Dance, worked at the famous Wanamaker department store in Philadelphia, toured with Buffalo Bill's Wild West show in Europe, and acted in Western movies; these, and other adventures, endowed him with a wider vision of the world. He, and tribal leaders who matured in the last century with a sense of tragic wisdom, might have warned the tribes to throw some of their casino millions to others as an association of power, and as an honorable mandate of sovereignty.

To endure the adversities of political lobbies the tribes must do more for others in the world than the government has done for them in the past. The rich casino tribes must demonstrate the power of their sovereignty to the world. Otherwise, the unresolved issues of state taxation, the enforcement of criminal statutes on reservations, and the resistance to casinos on reservation land could cause more contention among the tribes, communities near casinos, and state governments.

The Italian word casino means either "country house" or "gaming house," and "pleasure establishment." The definitions have varied over the years, but the sense of taboos over the pleasures of casinos has endured. Gambling is human, an ancient practice, and the outcome of the passion of chance could be determined in tribal casinos. Sovereignty has been won and lost, to be sure, over cards and other games of chance, but casinos have never been represented as the measure of tribal sovereignty. The future generations of the tribe may wonder what became of the billions and billions of dollars that were lost, and lost, and lost at the postindian pancasinos on reservations.

The tribes could name ambassadors to various nations and establish an international presence as a sovereign government; the creation of embassies would be a wiser test of sovereignty than casino riches with no honorable power. Then the tribal embassies could negotiate with casino monies the liberation of hundreds of stateless families in the world.

The liberation of Kurdish, Tibetan, Haitian, and other families, for instance, would sustain the moral traditions of tribal cultures. The relocation of these families to reservation communities would situate an undeniable tribal sovereignty and earn the international eminence of a government.

Casinos are the wages of wealth, morality, and sovereignty, but tribal courage and an international presence could secure more than the envies of casino riches and the limited sovereignty determined by federal courts and the government. Casino avarice with no moral traditions is a mean measure of tribal wisdom.

7

RADICAL DURANCE

The Vietnam War, and the horrors of racialism recounted in the literature of survivance, aroused the nation to remember the inseparable massacres at My Lai, Sand Creek, and Wounded Knee.

That narrative turn in consciousness, and federal legislation to transmute poverty in the nation, created the third historical nomination of tribal leaders by outsiders: the first was the simulation of tribal chiefs, the selection of *men* to negotiate agreements and treaties that served colonial and national territorial interests; the second was tied to literacy, the federal reorganization of tribal governments, relocation, and assimilation policies; the third was related to the revisions of tribal histories and federal poverty programs. At the same time, in the late sixties, there were simulated leaders in the cities who wore bone, beads, and leather, and strained to be the representations of traditional tribal cultures.

These leaders, the third nomination and simulation by outsiders, were discovered by the media; the first two nominations were personal encounters. The private, and the remembrance of the sacred, was overturned once more; the privacy of ceremonies became a simulation, and the absence of the tribal real became the real in the public media. The new simulated leaders in the cities had lost their sense of tribal privacy; they had encountered the unreal associations of institutions. These nominations were made much easier with the consumer sun dances, and some of these new tribal leaders were dressed to the simulations of photographs by Edward Curtis.

"Privacy is usually considered a moral interest of paramount importance. Its loss provokes talk of violation, harm, and loss of agency," wrote Julie Inness in *Privacy, Intimacy, and Isolation*. "Privacy is defined as a variety of freedom, a freedom that functions by granting the individual control over the division between the public and the private with respect to certain aspects of life."

There were other tribal simulations that touched the most conservative foundations, and there were diverse political interests in competition for federal funds, but liberal sentiments over the war and racial persecution were so intense that tribal leaders were named outright, as the chiefs once were by colonial fur traders in the eighteenth century.

The horrors of the war, racialism, the corruption of institutions, and the liberal furtherance of a cultural revolution induced an ironic tolerance of convicted criminals as leaders of community programs. This was a curious tolerance, to be sure, because some of these leaders had been in prison for crimes against people. These simulated leaders, and some were the kitschymen of resistance, had never been responsible to real tribal communities.

The chiefs nominated in the fur trade were men without tribal power; the chiefs lost the stories and the power of the tribe in the aesthetic association with colonial dominance. Some chiefs were mentioned in histories, others were wise enough to use their nomination as resistance, but most of these chiefs were the aesthetic inventions of dominance; they lost their sense of chance in stories and the shimmer of trickster survivance.

The chiefs of the fur trade and the kitschymen of the media are men without stories. Their considerations are causal and repetitious; at best, their stories serve the mere enterprise of resistance.

The kitschymen are the simulations of the media, the men with no real power of their own. Their speeches are not heard as leaders were heard in the past, and the associations of their resistance are an enterprise, not a real tribal discourse. The nomination of kitschymen in the media is the loss of tribal power, or the traditional separation of power is lost in the simulations of resistance. The menace of kitschymen causes the fear of violence, but fear is not a source of power in tribal communities. Most of these kitschymen are without imagination, and without stories; they must convince others that the *real* is more treacherous than their simulations in the media.

Violence is the "essence of power," observed Pierre Clastres in *Society Against the State*. The concern in tribal communities is the separation of power from institutions and "it is the very domain of speech that ensures the separation and draws the dividing line. By compelling the chief to move about in the area of speech alone, that is, the opposite of violence, the tribe makes certain that all things will remain in their place, that the axis of power will turn back exclusively to the social body, and that no displacement of forces will come to upset the social order."

Moreover, "the chief's obligation to speak, that steady flow of empty speech that he *owes* the tribe, is his infinite debt, the guarantee that prevents the man of speech from becoming a man of power."

The nomination of chiefs and kitschymen as speakers and leaders is the opposite of tribal power. Kitschymen are the dissociation of tribal discourse; they must pursue other simulations of power and dominance. The kitschyman in trickster stories would be summoned to an everlasting speech so that the tribe would not have to listen.

The American Indian Movement, a union of urban crossbloods, for the most part, was established in the late sixties. The radical leaders were nominated by the enterprise of resistance and discovered by the media; the simulations, at the time, became the absence of leadership in the sense that a simulation is the absence of the real. Some of these new chiefs had been in prison and had never been better paid for their resistance. Program grants, and other contributions, were new sources of influence in urban tribal communities.

Indians have been invented to represent the concerns and presentiments of each generation. Once more the media embraced the simulations of the tribes as the other, the outset of the postmodern antiselves of the nation; however, the new creases in coverage were uneven simulations that teased survivance over the manifest manners of dominance.

The Associated Press, for instance, reported that Dennis Banks, in 1982, would return to prison in South Dakota. He was wanted then on a fugitive warrant. "I am armed with whatever weapon," he said, "one of peace or one that will carry myself to the Great Spirit." Banks, at that time, was the chancellor of Daganawidah-Quetzalcoatl University, located near Davis, California. Governor Jerry Brown had denied his extradition to South Dakota. He served one year in prison and became a capitalist.

Paul Liberatore reported in the *San Francisco Chronicle* on 12 August 1988 that Banks was "no longer the angry young warrior." The radical seemed to be more mature, mellow, and credulous. "As you get older, you get wiser about how to solve things," said Banks. "You understand life better, the importance of it. Confrontation brings out the worst in everybody. Negotiation is a better way."

Russell Means, Clyde Bellecourt, Banks, and others were established media warriors at Wounded Knee. United Press International reported in front-page stories on 1 March 1973 that "members of the American Indian Movement held ten people hostage . . . at this Pine Ridge Reservation town where more than 200 Indians were massacred by Cavalry troops in 1890." The report was scandalous, the manifest manners of separatism, and the simulations of savagism and civilization. There were never hostages; the radical leaders were charged with conspiracy, but not kidnapping or any other crime associated with hostages.

Banks and Means were indicted for alleged violation of federal laws in connection with the occupation at Wounded Knee. The leaders were brought to trial but the case was dismissed because of government misconduct. Banks told the jurors in federal court about the sun dance, that "the piercing of the skin is a reminder to me that I truly owe myself to Mother Earth . . . and when the flesh was torn from me I suddenly realized what a great sin, what a great injustice, it would be to lose the Oglala Sioux religion."

Sun dances are ceremonies that honor the creation, spiritual visions, and the nerve of those who puncture the skin on their chest with wooden skewers; the skewers are tied to a sacred tree, and the sun dancers move in the circle of the sun until the skewers are torn from the flesh. The traditional sun dancers were the warriors of moral visions and silence. In the past decade some sun dances have become the consumer simulations of resistance; the kitschymen boast about their scars and dances.

Means, Bellecourt, Lehman Brightman, and others entered the circle of sun dancers, wrote Ed McGaa in the *Rainbow Tribe*, and observed a Catholic priest "just as we dancers were making our entry." He "stepped right in front of me in his black suit and waved a peace pipe. A confrontation took place during the recess period under the shade bower. I couldn't say anything while we were out in the Sun Dance arena as it wouldn't have been proper. Russ, Clyde, and Lehman came over to support me and warned the priest not to go back out into the dance arena. The priest then rushed to the microphone to stir up his followers, but he was sent packing and we went on with our ceremony without having to dilute it or cater to his beliefs. . . . Now it is a new time. There are literally hundreds of young, vibrant sun dancers, and traditionalism has swept the reservations."

The American Indian Movement, two decades after the occupation of Wounded Knee, is more kitsch and tired simulation than menace or moral tribal visions. The leaders are as close to retirement as those who funded their resistance enterprises and adventures. The church and state contribute to other causes now, and the media covers casinos, tribal sovereignty, and tribal court decisions with more interest than the activities of urban radical leaders and the kitschymen of the resistance enterprises.

"Basically, the world of kitsch is a world of aesthetic make-believe and self-deception," and "kitsch may be viewed as a reaction against the 'terror' of change and the meaninglessness of chronological time flowing from an unreal past into an equally unreal future," observed Matei Calinescu in *Five Faces of Modernity*. "Kitsch appears as an easy way of 'killing time,' as a pleasurable escape from the banality of both work and leisure. The fun of kitsch is just the other side of terrible and incomprehensible boredom." The kitschymen soothe the nostalgia for manifest manners and the melancholy of dominance.

Resistance is a simulation that supersedes the real in performance, but the tribal real is not an enterprise of resistance. The kitschymen are the simulations of banal spiritualism, the iterance of boredom, the closure of survivance, and the resistance enterprises of consumer sun dances.

Clyde Bellecourt was discovered by the media and established as a leader by foundations and government institutions. He could have been historical in the banal sense of time, causation, and aesthetic melancholy; instead, he became one of the kitschymen of resistance enterprises. Clearly, his nomination and media simulation as a leader were not based on violations of federal drug laws.

Bellecourt is a kitschyman, one of the most contumacious cross-blood radical simulations in the nation. He is a word warrior on commission, a man who has abused the honor of tribal communities to enhance his own simulations of pleasure and radical durance. The

most ambitious public records of his promotions are dominance, the
enterprise of his resistance. The arrogance of his presence must burden the most reasonable intimacies, the shadows in stories, and the
traces of humor that arise in conversations.

Bellecourt endures his own miseries, to be sure, and the causes of
his simulations are seldom invitational. He is represented by the institutions he accuses of conspiracies, and he is secure in a constitutional
democracy. Reported to be an invincible leader, he is the kitschyman
of liberal melancholy; however, he has never been elected to his public pose. He is the absence of the tribal leader in the simulations of
radical durance. Such a man must bear a serious vision, more than
mere confessions, conversions, and resistance enterprises could ever
reveal in the stories told to the media; otherwise, an undone vision
could be a treacherous pose, and a mission of dominance.

Newspapers have courted his simulation with recurrent tolerance
and the conceit of manifest manners. Very few writers have demonstrated the nerve to be as critical of the motivations of kitschymen and
the radical pose as they have been of elected officials and institutions.
Kim Ode, in this instance, is one of the differences in media coverage:
she touched on the simulation of dominance and the melancholy of
the American Indian Movement.

Bellecourt "has told his story so many times, a story that takes
him from the White Earth Indian Reservation to Wounded Knee to
federal prison and back to Franklin" Avenue, she reported in the
Minneapolis Star Tribune. "It unfolds as easily as a school teacher's
lesson, earnest yet having acquired a rehearsed quality over the years.

"Someday, his account of his more recent life as a cocaine addict
may take on the same rote nature. For now, though, he speaks. . . .
with more spontaneity, blurting details of mirrors and razor blades,
then proceeding haltingly, as if sifting the right words from kilos of
possibilities. He was convicted in April 1986 of selling LSD to under-
cover agents. He pleaded guilty inside the courtroom and claimed

entrapment outside it. He served twenty-two months of a five-year federal prison term and emerged determined to improve the life of Indian children.

"Bellecourt may have changed, but not everyone is buying it. Those who dislike him refuse to speak on the record, saying that they fear reprisals. Word of a newspaper article ignites the grapevine and the telephone rings with anonymous voices, all of whom identify themselves as American Indians, urging caution."

Joseph Geshick was not hesitant to make critical observations in a newspaper article: "Clyde Bellecourt instigated two ugly actions in North Twin Lake," northern Wisconsin, "during the spearfishing season," he wrote in the *Native American Press*. He intimidated a woman, and he provoked "the treaty protesters in complete violation of the rules set down by the spearfishing organization." Geshick wrote that Bellecourt was disgraceful and arrogant because only a "fool would possibly jeopardize the safety of people at a boat landing, and possibly jeopardize even the treaties as well. Clyde was guilty of racism as well."

"Clyde was recently a guest at the American Indian Services. He apparently was intent on tearing down the self-esteem of a young client," wrote Geshick. "Clyde likes to play word games to discourage and destroy others' egos, it must make him feel powerful. Fortunately, he is not richly endowed with mental ability. The fine young Anishinabe man, more intelligent and quicker thinking, quickly replied in this verbal duel, 'At least I've never dealt drugs.'

"Clyde has none of the qualities required to qualify as a leader of any Anishinabe people. He is not a fair person. He tells lies with an ease that has to be seen to believe. He steals the credit of many hard working people, as if he alone were responsible for all the work done on an issue. He does not have proper respect for other Indians."

Bellecourt is critical of reservation casinos, but he is cautious to land his criticism in remote places. The casino industry is "a major conspiracy against Indian people," he said at the Round Lake Reservation. Federal agencies know about the corruption on reservations. "They'll come in and they'll say that organized crime has control over your reservation, over your resources, over your housing, over your education, over everything that you do as Indian people," reported the *County Ledger Press* of Balsam Lake, Wisconsin.

"I have come here for the children," he said at the Round Lake Reservation. "I want these children to have a good education. I want them to learn about their culture, their tradition. I want them to grow up to be proud of who they are."

Bellecourt is the prater of continuous conspiracies; nonetheless, he wonders what the government does about corruption on reservations. Others must wonder about his association with hallucinogenic drugs and why law enforcement agencies did not investigate and arrest him sooner. Could he have been protected in his enterprise of resistance? Conspiracies are the simulations of manifest manners and the literature of dominance.

Bellecourt was charged with the sale of hallucinogenic drugs worth thousands of dollars; a federal grand jury indicted him on nine felony counts in December 1986. Five others were charged in the same indictment. He pleaded guilty to one count of drug distribution as part of a negotiated plea bargain.

Kevin Diaz reported in the *Minneapolis Star Tribune* that Bellecourt appeared "contrite" in court, but he turned his stories outside. "The whole thing was set up by the government," said Bellecourt. "They've spent hundreds of thousands of dollars in surveillance in the last year. They've been trailing me for the last eighteen years, since the founding of AIM," the American Indian Movement.

Bellecourt was sentenced to five years in prison for the distribution of drugs. Randy Furst reported that Federal District Judge Paul Magnuson "had great respect for what Bellecourt had done for the Indian community and society as a whole, but referred to the 'devastating crime' he had committed in distributing 'one of the most danger-ous drugs.'" Bellecourt was allowed to attend a sun dance ceremony in Arizona before he surrendered to federal authorities to begin his prison sentence.

"Supporters sat in the courtroom as two of Bellecourt's long-time associates, attorney Doug Hall and Paul Boe of the American Lutheran Church, urged leniency, although deploring his involve-ment in drug sales," reported Furst in the *Minneapolis Star Tribune.* "Boe cited his 'dedication to his people' in confronting injustice."

Special Agent Michele Leonhart of the Drug Enforcement Admin-istration testified that she had been involved in the investigation of drug trafficking activities of Clyde Bellecourt since the winter of 1984. Arrangements were made through Bellecourt on March 21, 1985, "to purchase 5,000 hits of LSD at the Perkins Restaurant located on Riverside and 27th Avenue South, Minneapolis, Minnesota." Two months earlier, "Agent Stevens and I drove to the parking lot located to the east of 2534 Ogema Place and waited for Bellecourt." The two agents, Stevens and Leonhart, "discussed purchasing 2,000 hits of LSD from Bellecourt. Agent Stevens asked Bellecourt what color the LSD would be and Bellecourt replied that the LSD would probably be 'green pyramids' and that he was going to go check on it. Bellecourt explained that if 'the guy' was home, Bellecourt could get the LSD right away. Bellecourt agreed to go check on the LSD and return in one half hour."

Clyde Bellecourt was arrested on December 23, 1985, in Minne-apolis. Kenneth VandeSteeg, narcotics officer, testified that he had participated in a surveillance of Bellecourt, "prior to being stopped and arrested" on a warrant for "violation of federal narcotics laws."

"Did you recover certain items from his person?"

"Yes."

"Did you recover a quantity of cash?"

"Yes. There was approximately $804 in currency. There was zigzag wrappers cigarette wrappers, miscellaneous papers, identification, and one marijuana cigarette that I retrieved from a, I think it was, a pack of Salem cigarettes. There was one plastic baggie, also, in his pocket with what appeared to me to be marijuana residue. And a small bindle with powder traces in it." Bellecourt, he said, also "had some grass in his boot."

John Lee, Assistant United States Attorney, argued that the defendant should be detained because of his previous criminal record. Douglas Hall, one of the lawyers who defended Bellecourt, objected to the police report because it contained misdemeanors.

Lee pointed out that "Bellecourt's criminal history does include a felony conviction in 1954 in connection with a robbery charge. That in connection with the sentence he received on that conviction, his parole was violated in 1958 and 1960. That he was convicted in 1971 on a simple assault charge. It's my further offer of proof that Mr. Bellecourt is a traveler abroad and has traveled abroad on a number of occasions. It's a further offer of proof that in the past year in the course of investigation, the agents were unable to determine a permanent address for Mr. Bellecourt; and, in fact, located him only with great difficulty. . . .

"Further offer of proof, that although Mr. Bellecourt claims employment with the Jobs Training Program Office at the Little Earth Housing Project, that appears to be only a place where he obtains his messages and that the agents repeatedly were unable to locate him there during business hours and that the personnel there indicated that he very infrequently was present at that office. . . ."

Douglas Hall presented the testimony of many people who had worked with Bellecourt in community programs, and "we would ask them directly their opinions of whether or not he's dangerous in the community and whether or not there is any danger that he would abscond and not appear."

Bellecourt declared in an affidavit his honorable reasons to travel to the Sun Dance at Big Mountain in Arizona. The government tried to prevent his travel because of alleged "escalating conflict . . . between the Navaho and Hopi Indians." Bellecourt pointed out that the description was not "an accurate statement of the situation."

He declared that from "*my* times in the Big Mountain area, it is my personal observation and belief that there is NOT escalating conflict between the two tribes in the joint use area, but that the contrary is true. Steps have been taken to resolve the differences between the tribes and with the government in a peaceful and constructive way.

"It is true that there has been a lot of recent publicity surrounding the issue of forced relocation of Navaho and a lesser number of Hopi from the places they have lived for centuries or years. But that publicity, in my observation, has not anticipated any violent confrontation between the Indians and government and has been largely sympathetic to the Indians who are subject to the 1974 federal relocation legislation. The Navaho and Hopi have traditionally been some of the most peaceful, least warlike cultures on this earth. . . ." Bellecourt turns to manifest manners in certain situations; his reason ranges from federal conspiracies to a utopian peace.

"The past three Sun Dances at Big Mountain have had no political incidents or clashes whatsoever. In fact, the tribal councils of both tribes and the B.I.A. recognize the sacred nature of the Sun Dance ceremony and have never interfered with it in any way.

"The Sun Dance will be held on lands about twenty miles away from the survival camp near Big Mountain. It is usually held in August of each year, but was specifically scheduled" earlier this year "in order that it be completed *before* any forced relocation might occur. The Sun Dance is such a holy and life-affirming ceremony, that to engage in any strife or violent acts during it or immediately following it would be extremely sacrilegious. . . .

"No alcohol, drugs, weapons or violence of any kind are tolerated at a Sun Dance. . . . It is my sincere belief that there will be no strife, conflict, political activity or violence of any kind at the Sun Dance, whether relating to the forced relocation controversy or not. Peoples of Hopi and Navaho tribes will participate in the ceremonies side by side with Lakota and other Indian peoples from throughout the country.

"I personally promise this court that I will not become involved in any controversy or strife—if any should somehow occur—while I am present at the Sun Dance. I make this promise out of religious conviction first, and also out of respect for this court. . . .

"It is very important to me personally to be able to attend the Sun Dance. My desire to go arises purely from my spiritual and religious beliefs. I have participated in these ceremonies each year since 1973. . . . For me, the Sun Dance has been very important in helping me win my battle with alcohol. I had been through alcohol treatment programs without success, but was able to gain and maintain sobriety since the first Sun Dance in 1973. I also need to participate before I go to prison; it is a religious ceremony that is not available in prison. . . .

"This is also an especially important year since my oldest son, Little Crow, will be participating in the Sun Dance for the fourth and final year of this dance. This is a ceremony where he will become a young man. And he and my entire family will need this ceremony to help him and them as I leave to go to prison," declared Bellecourt.

"Most of all, I ask the court to allow me to exercise this last important religious rite with my family before I go to prison where such exercise will be impossible. This court has recognized that I am neither a violent person nor a risk to flee. The government's fears over the political land disputes in the area should be allayed: those disputes are not to be blindly lumped together with the Indian nations' (and my own) exercise of sincere and deeply held religious beliefs."

Bellecourt was allowed to attend the Sun Dance at Big Mountain in

Arizona. He surrendered to authorities on time and served less than two years in federal prison. The court must have believed his stories about tribal religious experiences.

Joseph Geshick has the courage to remember other stories about the Sun Dance and Bellecourt. He wrote in the *Native American Press* that he had seen "Mathew King do the announcing during Sundances and treaty meetings." He "was a very intelligent, honest elder of the Lakota; expert in treaty law interpretation and was always willing to share his knowledge. Mathew noticed a bag appear at Clyde Bellecourt's feet while Clyde was speaking. Clyde finished and left. Mathew King picked up the bag and sniffed it. He immediately walked to the microphone and announced, 'Clyde Bellecourt, you dropped your bag of dope. Would you please come back to the speaker's stand and retrieve it.' Clyde did not come back and claim the lost item."

8

EPILOGUE

"I saw the Sacs & Foxes at the Statehouse" in Boston, wrote Ralph Waldo Emerson in his *Journals* on 2 November 1837. "Edward Everett addressed them & they replied. One chief said 'They had no land to put their words upon, but they were nevertheless true.' "

Emerson noted that "it is right & natural that the Indian should come & see the civil White man, but his was hardly genuine but a show so we were not parties but spectators." The audience of the other had been reversed in a generation. Lewis and Clark wanted to be *seen* by the tribes. Emerson was a spectator, *unseen* at an overture of a chief who had come to *see* civilization. In that generation the tribes had been decimated by diseases; the cruelties of civilization had dispossessed the tribes of their land, but not their stories. The shadows of their words, the hermeneutics of survivance, are forever true on the land stolen from the tribes.

The selections from *The Journals of Lewis and Clark* were edited by Bernard DeVoto. He based his edition on the seven volume *Original Journals of the Lewis and Clark Expedition*, edited by Reuben Gold Thwaites. "When Thwaites published the journals, he was obliged to reproduce them exactly and to supply editorial emendations. He indicated missing letters and words by printing them in brackets; I have retained almost all such emendations," wrote DeVoto. "The spellings of the original are a large part of its charm, and I have not changed them at all. For the most part too I have retained the original punctuation; occasionally a deletion I have made has required me to insert or delete or change a mark of punctuation in order to retain the sense."

Lewis and Clark "were obviously unawed and unafraid, but they were also obviously friendly and fair, scrupulously honest, interested, understanding, courteous, and respectful," observed DeVoto. "That last quality must be insisted on, for rare as honesty and fairness were in the white American's dealing with Indians, they were commoner than respect. Lewis and Clark respected the Indians' personal dignity, their rituals, their taboos, their religious thinking, indeed the full content of their thought."

Lieutenant William Reynolds wrote to his sister Lydia on 7 November 1841 that an "Indian pilot was sent out to us, who brought us safely in, and we anchored in the quiet and beautiful cover where the shipwrecked ones had found a refuge, overjoyed to take our brothers by the hand and happy to find for ourselves a peaceful resting place, after the nervous and harrowing excitement of the past days." The *Peacock* sank in the mouth of the Columbia River near Astoria. Reynolds described the incident with minimal sentiment, but he was not disposed to *respect* the tribal pilot who brought his schooner safely to anchor. His letters were published by the Naval Institute Press in *Voyage to the Southern Ocean*. "I must not forget to say that the men of the *Peacock* behaved like *men* during the whole of the danger and that order and discipline were preserved to a degree that reflects credit upon them all."

Francis Paul Prucha wrote in the introduction to *Americanizing the American Indians* that "even more important than private property or citizenship under American laws was education.... Education for patriotic American citizenship became the new panacea, and from 1887 to the end of the century it was one of the major concerns of the reformers and of the Bureau of Indian Affairs. The proposal of the 1888 Lake Mohonk Conference for a universal government school system for the Indians was taken up by the Commissioner of Indian Affairs in 1889, and a solid start was made in providing schools for Indians that would parallel the public school system and would turn out the same end product: patriotic American citizens."

Merrill Gates, the nineteenth century reformer, president of Amherst College, and member of the Board of Indian Commissioners, reasoned that "Christian missionaries plunge into these reservations, struggle with the mass of evil there, and feeling that bright children can be best educated in the atmosphere of civilization, they send to Eastern institutions these Indian children plucked like fire-stained brands from the reservations. They are brought to our industrial training schools. The lesson taught by the comparison of their photographs when they come and when they go is wonderful."

Luther Standing Bear was one of these "fire-stained brands from the reservation." He was educated at the federal school near Carlisle, Pennsylvania. "At last the train arrived at a junction where we were told we were at the end of our journey. Here we left the train and walked about two miles to the Carlisle Barracks," wrote Standing Bear in *My People the Sioux*. "Soon we came to a big gate in a great high wall. The gate was locked, but after quite a long wait, it was unlocked and we marched in through it. I was the first boy inside. At that time I thought nothing of it, but now I realize that I was the first Indian boy to step inside the Carlisle Indian School grounds."

Captain Richard Pratt, superintendent of the first government school at Carlisle, wrote that the Indian "must have something more than Indian school, more than school of any sort: he must have experience." His notions were published in the *Proceedings of the Eleventh Annual Meeting of the Lake Mohonk Conference of Friends of the Indian* in 1893, and edited by Prucha in *Americanizing the American Indian*. "I have grown to believe in every fibre of me that

we wrong ourselves and the Indians when we build them up as tribes, and to know that we do this when we plant our schools in the tribes, where their greatest influence is to hold the Indian to the tribe; that, by spending all our energies and efforts to keep them tribes and separate communities, we but perpetuate bureau control and prolong missionary fields, but grow up precious little of the independent manhood fibre required for success in our civilization." Pratt believed that tribal schools, or schools on reservations, were "largely a waste of public money."

William Hagan pointed out in *American Indians* that Pratt established the best known boarding school in 1879. "In charge of Indian prisoners in Florida, he was impressed by their adaptability and helped secure admission for some of them to Hampton Institute, a private school for Negroes. At Carlisle, which was supported entirely by federal funds, Pratt introduced the outing system. Coming at the end of the Indian youth's stay at Carlisle, this involved placing the mature student for a period of as much as three years with one of the rural families near Carlisle. Pratt was a strong advocate of assimilation and a bitter critic of contract schools maintained by church groups with government subsidy." Pratt argued that reservations should be abolished and "Indians completely integrated into white society."

"Guard the rights of the Indian, but for his own good break up his reservations," wrote Merrill Gates. "Let in the light of civilization. Plant in alternate sections or townships white farmers, who will teach him by example." Prucha selected his essay, "Land and Law as Agents in Educating Indians," which was first published in *Seventeenth Annual Report of the Board of Indian Commissioners.*

Larzer Ziff observed that the absence of the tribes "rather than their presence" posed the "greatest danger" to the expedition of Lewis and Clark. Ziff has written an outstanding interpretation of intellectual histories that both discerns and *respects* the imagination and survivance of Native American Indians. "As I made my way into the writings of the age, I was struck by the powerful drift from immanence to representation in both literature and society, from a common belief that reality resided in a region beneath appearance and beyond manipulation to the belief that it could be constructed and so made identical with appearance," he wrote in *Writing in the New Nation*.

"The message that flowed from the new Americans to the Indians bound the receivers to the senders' goods, government, and language. To be sure, an important strand of European thought sought to reverse this direction, insisting that the Indian in the purity of his separation from the artifices of civilization and his immersion in a life led in response to the rhythms of nature could be seen as a guide to the rejuvenation of an exhausted European culture," wrote Ziff. "Although the noble savage who filled this role was a creation of social philosophers, once he existed on the page those who responded to his symbolic significance also located him in the life."

The postindian antecedes the postmodern condition; the resistance of the tribes to colonial inventions and representations envisioned the ironies of histories, narrative discourse, and cultural diversities. The postindian mien is survivance over dominance; the postmodern is the discourse of histories over metanarratives.

The Indian became the homogenous name for thousands of distinct tribal cultures. The Anishinaabe were named the Chippewa. The Dakota were named the Sioux. Other tribal names are colonial inventions sustained in the literature of dominance. That some postindians renounce the inventions and final vocabularies of manifest manners is the advance of survivance hermeneutics.

Paula Gunn Allen, for instance, created the word gynocracies with a different meaning than gynecocracies. "Tribal gynocracies," she wrote in *The Sacred Hoop*, "prominently feature even distribution of goods among all members of the society on the grounds that First

Mother enjoined cooperation and sharing on all her children. . . . But colonial attempts at cultural gynocide notwithstanding, there were and are gynocracies—that is, woman-centered tribal societies in which matrilocality, matrifocality, matrilinearity, maternal control of household goods and resources, and female deities of the magnitude of the Christian God were and are present and active features of traditional tribal life."

The ventures of imagination, shadow remembrance, survivance hermeneutics, comic turns of creation, tragic wisdom in the ruins of representation, transformations in trickster stories, and individual visions, were one and the same themes in classical literature; however, the surveillance of the social sciences and the invention of the other concealed the genius of natural reason, the ironies of tribal imagination, and the shimmer of survivance stories. The tribal other became the double other of surveillance, separation, and individuation; the final vocabularies and double other of the antiselves of dominance. At the same time the romance of the noble savage was borrowed to counter the cruelties of civilization.

Michel Serres considered the conservative nature of surveillance and observation. "The human sciences are surveillance; the exact sciences are an observation. The first are as old as our myths; the others, new, were born with us, and are only as old as our history. Myth, theater, representation, and politics do not teach us how to observe; they commit us to a surveillance." His essay, "Panoptic Theory," was published in *The Limits of Theory*, edited by Thomas Kavanagh. The objectivism of the object world becomes a virtue in his interpretations. "The exact sciences were formed with the emergence of the object," he wrote. "The sciences that have no objects know only the methods of the detective or the policeman; they are a part of myth. Objective knowledge makes up our present history; the human sciences, which are ancient, take us back to mythology. Observation weaves in the light of day what surveillance undoes in the dark of the night."

Jean-François Lyotard would advance the literature of survivance over manifest manners and dominance. He argued in *The Postmodern Explained* that "it should be made clear that it is not up to us to *provide reality*, but to invent illusions to what is conceivable." He pointed out that the "postmodern artist or writer is in the position of a philosopher: the text he writes or the work he creates is not in principle governed by preestablished rules and cannot be judged according to a determinant judgment, by the application of given categories to this text or work. Such rules and categories are what the work or text is investigating."

Vassilis Lambropoulos observed in *The Rise of Eurocentrism* that postmodernism "is not ignorant or innocent of history but rather sees it as the total, synchronic, undifferentiated presence and availability of tradition. While modernist artwork is about itself and seeks redemption from history through form, the postmodernist is about tradition and surrounds itself happily with history; the former strives to establish its own code, the latter thrives on borrowed codes."

The postindians are the simulations of survivance; they bear the postmodern presence of tribal traditions and histories in the instance of stories. Alas, surveillance is a modernist separation of tribal imagination and the concoction of the other in the ruins of representation. Postindians discover the survivance of their others and their double others in libraries. "The postmodernist work reflects the experience of the library, where everything is available and within reach but placed in an order that eliminates any sense of hierarchical history," wrote Lambropoulos.

Heard stories and narrative histories are suspensive; in that sense, both suspense and suspension, readers are the double others of their own fear in the silence of libraries. Postindian narratives are suspensive; the shadows, and presence of tribal traditions, have no hierarchies in libraries, because interpretations are signatures of imagination and the liberation of narratives. These are not the binaries of savagism and civilization; rather, the paradoxes of narrative fear, the suspension of domination, and survivance hermeneutics.

"The fear of writing is the fear of language's otherness," wrote Stephen Moore in *Mark and Luke in Poststructuralist Perspectives.* "It is symptomatic of another fear, loss of individual selfhood." The heard is creation, our presence; the written narrative is mute, and "my mother tongue is always an other's tongue. Language's alterity, ever threatening to dispossess me of my self, has its emblem in the exteriority of writing. My writing is always unmoored from me, even when it bears my signature. It begins outside me, is funneled through me, and goes on talking without me. I fade behind it and slip beneath it."

Trickster narratives are suspensive, an ironic survivance; trickster metaphors are contradictions not representations of culture. The peripatetic trickster is a deverbative narrative in translation, a noun derived from a verb; an elusive name that bears the shadows of the heard in active narratives and the tension of nominalism.

"The relation between noun and verb most clearly illustrates the way in which languages manipulate the universe," observed Claude Hagège in *The Dialogic Species.* "An ancient antagonism exists between those who assign priority to the verb and those who assign it to the noun."

The shadows of the heard in trickster narratives are intransitive; the trickster as a noun is causal representation in translation. The presence of the active trickster in the heard is the deverbative other in written narratives. Naanabozho, the shadow name of the trickster in the language of the Anishinaabe, is an ironic creator and, in the same instance, the contradiction of creation. The representations of his name are transformations in the natural world; his father is the wind, and his brother is a stone. Nouns and names are simulations of the other in translation.

The intransitive motion of shadows, and the presence of shadows in the silence of names, is a source of remembrance and survivance hermeneutics. The sensations of shadows in trickster narratives are neither closure nor menace in the absence of light. The motions of shadows are not heard in natural reason as the structural archetypes of the unconscious. Natural reason would seldom separate or divaricate trickster and creation narratives from shadows and dreams and the ecstasies of shamans.

"A man who is possessed by his shadow is always standing in his own light and falling into his own traps," observed Carl Jung in *Four Archetypes.* To construe that creation is an established pattern of representation, and to impose archetypes on tribal remembrance and narratives, is to sustain manifest manners and the literature of dominance. Jung reasoned that if "we take the trickster as a parallel of the individual shadow, then the question arises whether that trend toward meaning, which we saw in the trickster myth, can also be observed in the subjective and personal shadow."

John Lyons argued in *Natural Language and Universal Grammar* that the noun is the "one substantive universal of syntactic theory," and the "verbal complex" in some languages "may stand as a 'one-word sentence.' "

The nouns practice to be subjects and objects in sentences; the verbs are clever and independent, the shadows that would become names. "Nouns are primary, in the sense that they are linked referentially with 'things,' " wrote Lyons. In that sense, nouns "determine the selection of verbs" in sentences. "Since the 'things' referred to in utterances are often physically present in the situations in which the utterances are spoken."

The tricksters in narratives, however, are the metaphors of creation that determine the nouns; presence, and situations of the heard, are perceived in the references of an utterance. Unblest in translation, the trickster becomes a nominal silhouette, the other as a thing or object, in the literature of dominance.

Trickster narratives, that natural reach of creation, and shadows of remembrance, are causal contradictions in translation. The action, names, and pronouns in narratives are linear in structure, but not in the dimensions of imagination. Trickster narratives are read as linear translations, but the action was heard as holophrastic.

"The point of view which defines causes is relative, restrictive, and finite," wrote John William Miller in *The Paradox of Cause and Other Essays*. "Causes demand the incomplete. *Causes demand relative disorder.*" The paradox is that cause is both *universal* and *restricted*; cause is both anarchy and unity. "Cause pretends to offer us unity and order: but what makes actual causal intelligibility possible is disorder, finitude, restrictive; and what makes unity possible is the cancellation of that very disorder, finitude, and restriction."

The trickster is heard as natural reason, presence and absence, creation and ruin, anarchy and unity, but the narratives are read as causal simulations; the trickster is heard and mute, active and nominal, but the rush is incoherence.

"Cause is a dynamic concept because it describes an ideal, the ideal of the intelligibility of nature," wrote Miller. "For nature is in large part a mystery, and causal coherence is but one of the keys to its progressive solution. If we attempt to make this rule of process a character of a supposedly finished world, we can no longer define the rule."

Naanabozho would mimic but never concede the coherence of other worlds, and so the trickster continues the causal contradictions of presence and absence in a narrative that has no mechanisms of representation.

"There is no other world, and certainly no other causally ordered world," argued Miller. "In a word, the universality of cause does not imply mechanism; indeed it is just the *necessity of cause which is the ground of the refutation of mechanism.*"

Nominal tricksters are silhouettes in most commercial literature, the concoctions of the other rather than causal contradictions. Coyote simulations, the kitschy crusts of the deverbative trickster, are the mechanisms of consumer representations.

"In the beginning, there was just the water," said the narrator at the beginning and the end of *Green Grass, Running Water*, a comic novel by Thomas King. So, there was a coyote, and there was nothing, and these coyote stories, laced to pronominal histories, are at the water margin, that littoral of trickster survivance in literature.

The Lone Ranger, Ahab, Ishmael, Hawkeye, Robinson Crusoe, Changing Woman, Ahdamn, Mary Rowlandson, Henry Dawes, John Collier, Charlie Catlain, "Nasty" Bumppo, Coyote, and others come together with brand names in comic modernism to hear trickster stories about Moby-Jane and the Great Black Whale.

The stories count on one of the common representations of the trickster, that wild coyote with a coat of modernism; the cosmopolitan coyote is both unity and anarchy and reaches to be heard in this new novel by the author of *Medicine River*.

"My responsibilities are to the story and to the people from whom I get some of the stories," King told Jace Weaver in *Publishers Weekly*. "I like to hear my characters talking. I like to hear their voices. Although I greatly admire writers like N. Scott Momaday, who can go for pages and never have anyone say anything, I'd go nuts if I couldn't hear my characters speak."

Lionel, for instance, who sells televisions and stereos in the city, returned to the reserve and was treated to a new recipe, Tortino de Carciofi with Ribollita, that his mother prepared from an Italian cookbook. "What is it?" asked Lionel.

"Vegetable soup and an artichoke omelet."

"Where'd you get the artichokes?"

"I had to substitute."

"So, what's in it now?"

"Elk."

King said that his next novel is "less comic." He is "trying to move away from a culturally specific area completely." The Indians "aren't identified by tribe, for instance, and as a matter of fact, they're not even much identified by geographic area." That his characters are pantribal would be more obvious to some readers than others; those who search for authentic tribal representations would be concerned that the author has not served the literature of dominance. "I really don't care about the white audiences. They don't have an understanding of the intricacies of Native life, and I don't think they're much interested in it, quite frankly."

Houghton Mifflin Company, the publishers of *Green Grass, Running Water*, released a promotional interview with the author. King said, "I don't remember knowing another Indian until I got to college. My father was Cherokee out of Oklahoma, but he took off when I was about five, and we never saw him again. My mother is part Greek and part German, and she raised us by herself. . . . Actually, the ten years I spent at the University of Lethbridge working with Blackfoot and Cree people provided me with the basis for much of my fiction."

The conventions of travel literature bear the causal contradictions of discoveries, translation, narrative representations of the other, and the simulations of dominance. "Travel literature was involved in the development of many new kinds of writing," wrote Mary Campbell in *The Witness and the Other World*. Travel writing "is implicated in the origins of anthropology, it is also implicated in the origins of the modern novel, the renewal of heroic romance, and the foundations of scientific geography."

François-René de Chateaubriand, for instance, construed the "noble savage" as the double other of a melancholy civilization in the early nineteenth century. That romantic simulation of nature, and the contradictions of tribal individualism, have endured in the literature of discoveries and domination.

"As I open my story, I cannot stifle a feeling of shame," wrote Chateaubriand in *René*. "The peace in your hearts, respected elders, and the calm of nature all about me make me blush for the disorder and turmoil of my soul." René encountered the Natchez, and was "obliged to take a wife in order to conform to the Indian customs; but he did not live with her. His melancholy nature drew him constantly away into the depths of the woods. There he would spend entire days in solitude, a savage among the savages."

Chateaubriand discovered the mother of nature and "primitive liberty" in his simulations of the tribes in the New World. He, and countless other writers since the nineteenth century, have sustained their melancholy, and their leisure composure with readers, in the notions of the other as the solace of nature.

Chateaubriand wrote that the ideal savage "wanted freedom from dependence, wanted to be nothing but himself, not to have to dissimulate, hide his feelings, flatter, work for mercenary ends," observed Gerald Izenberg in *Impossible Individuality*. "European man, however, had learned another side of freedom; independence meant detachment from limits—familial, political, divine—and the next step was for the self to fill the space of possibility left when all limitations were seen as illegitimate. In the moment of consciousness, that step felt like ecstasy, an explosion of the kind that drove Chateaubriand from tree to tree in the American forests shouting the absence of restraints, taking untold liberties of behavior, feeling godlike in his sense of possibility."

The tribes have been burdened ever since with the narrative simulations of mother nature and the noble other as the unmeant sources of liberation from urban civilization. Such ecstasies, of course, become the romantic literature of dominance.

The casinos on reservations are the sources of riches and the absence of political power. The Mohawks, for instance, are divided over the operation of casinos on tribal reservation land. "Some Indians fear an invasion of disruptive neon-lit businesses and organized crime," reported The *New York Times*. "Others say gambling engenders a fast-money mentality at odds with traditional Mohawk values. Still others contend casinos will infringe Mohawk sovereignty by opening the reservation to state police officers, gambling inspectors," and other state and federal agencies. "A wild card in the gambling debate is a shadowy group known as the Warrior Society. Its members, whose numbers are not publicly known, promote a militant brand of nationalism that advocates reclaiming Mohawk land and opposes government intervention on the reservation, which they call Akwesasne. They have supported gambling as a means of giving Mohawks economic power." The Warrior Society is opposed to casino compacts with the state because such agreements would allow inspectors and police on sovereign tribal land.

"Gambling breaks down our cultural values," Chief Jake Swamp told The *New York Times*. He said he was opposed to gambling on the reservation. "And what I hear from people is that they are not going to take it any longer."

These conditions, and resistance on other reservations, are not the simulations of survivance; rather, the riches could move the most envious to violence. The literature of dominance has sustained the use of separation and violence in the past; in that sense, antisemitism and antitribalism are comparable detractions. "Antisemitism reached its climax when Jews had similarly lost their public functions and their influence, and were left with nothing but their wealth," observed Hannah Arendt in *Antisemitism*.

"Arendt insists that we can take no comfort in traditional concepts or expectations, that the radical novelty—the radical evil—of contemporary events requires a new kind of thinking," wrote Jeffrey Isaac in *Arendt, Camus, and Modern Rebellion*. "The events of the mid-twentieth century leave Arendt with a profound sense that the political world is in shambles. Far from the spirit of optimism, she suggests that perhaps the most appropriate response to the wreckage produced by the angel of history is humble repentance."

Barrett Mandel argued that in "autobiography, unlike fiction, we expect the work to embody, even in its illusion, the truth of the life of the writer." His essay, "Full of Life Now," was published in *Autobiography*, edited by James Olney. "Language creates illusions that tell the truth. The process of language constantly makes the discovery of truth possible because all language is rooted in human *being* and culture, so that even lies are anchored in being and contain the possibility of their own revelations. . . . If an autobiographer tells many lies, his words will eventually reveal him as one who means something other than what he says."

Arnold Krupat proposed that "while modern Western autobiography has been essentially metonymic in orientation, Native American autobiography has been and continues to be persistently synecdochic, and that the preference for synecdochic models of the self has relations to the oral techniques of information transmission typical of Native American culture." His essay, "Native American Autobiography," was published in *American Autobiography*, edited by Paul John Eakin.

Krupat seemed to assume that the "synecdochic models" revealed in the text are representations of tribal cultures outside of the text, and that the constituents of the synecdoche are not determined by interpretation, translation, and the philosophies of grammar.

The constituents of synecdoche and metaphor are ascertained by narrative interpretations and deconstructions; the immanence of tribal stories is not inclusive in literary interpretation. The tribe could be the mere part, the absence of the other, but not the silence, and an individual vision could be more inclusive than entire communities. The inventions of the other, and the antiselves, are the suspensive constituents of the synecdoche.

The autobiographical narrative must be ironic; otherwise some narratives would be more natural and essential than others. Shadow words and nicknames are survivance stories that seem to have an unstated presence in narratives; the reader hears the shadow stories. The synecdochic conversions in narratives are no more than narratives, and the interpretations are narratives, not real tribal cultures.

The dominance of discoveries and academic associations belie the sources of tribal narratives; silence, of course, is an unnatural survivance in literature, but surveillance, and too much observance, abrogates the narrative rights of tribal consciousness. Joseph Campbell, for instance, was so impressed with Jamake Highwater that his mere association became a mythic truth. Campbell, who had been enraptured by tribal cultures as a child, wrote to Highwater that he and his wife "spent an elegant afternoon" viewing "your two television creations, *The Primal Mind* and *Native Land*. . . . I think it so important: the work that you are doing [on the renewal of Native American consciousness]! And I take great satisfaction in the knowledge that my own work has in some way contributed to its realization." His letter was published in *A Fire in the Mind: The Life of Joseph Campbell* by Stephen and Robin Larsen.

Highwater nurtured his associations with notable scholars, artists, and publishers. "Joseph Campbell tells us that 'it is a curious characteristic of our unformed species that we live and model our lives through acts of make-believe.' We are myth makers," Highwater asserted in *Shadow Show: An Autobiographical Insinuation*. "We are the legenders. Of all the animals we alone are capable of dreaming ourselves into existence." Myth maker, indeed, and then the *insinuations* were uncovered in his own trickster narratives. Jack Anderson, the columnist, reported that Highwater "lied repeatedly about many details of his life." Indian leaders "Vine Deloria Jr. and Hank Adams say flatly that Highwater is not an Indian."

Index

CPSIA information can be obtained
at www.ICGtesting.com
Printed in the USA
LVHW041728020819
626322LV00014B/246/P